STAR WARS®

CHARACTER ENCYCLOPEDIA

Written by **Simon Beecroft**

CONTENTS

WHO PLANNED THE Rebel assault on the first Death Star? Which surly alien lost an arm in a Mos Eisley cantina? The *Star Wars* galaxy is full of heroes, villains, aliens, creatures, and droids. All have played their part—large or small—in the momentous events of the dying days of the Galactic Republic, the battles of the Clone Wars, and the desperate resistance against the Empire.

FINDING A CHARACTER
Look up characters alphabetically by their first name or title, or use the index on page 206.

2-1B 4
4-LOM 5
8D8 6
Aayla Secura 7
Acklay 8
Adi Gallia 9
Admiral Ackbar 10
Admiral Ozzel 11
Admiral Piett 12
Agen Kolar 13
Anakin Skywalker 14
AT-AT Pilot 15
AT-ST Pilot 16
Aurra Sing 17
A-wing Pilot 18
B'omarr Monk 19
Bail Organa 20
Bantha 21
Baron Papanoida 22
Barriss Offee 23
Battle Droid 24
Beru Lars 25
Bib Fortuna 26
Boba Fett 27
Boga 28
Boss Nass 29
Bossk 30
Boushh 31
Bultar Swan 32
Buzz Droid 33

C-3PO 34
Captain Antilles 35
Captain Needa 36
Captain Panaka 37
Captain Typho 38
Chancellor Valorum 39
Chewbacca 40
Chi Eekway Papanoida 41
Chief Chirpa 42
Cin Drallig 43
Cliegg Lars 44
Clone Pilot 45
Clone Trooper (Phase I) 46
Clone Trooper (Phase II) 47
Coleman Trebor 48
Colo Claw Fish 49
Commander Bacara 50
Commander Bly 51
Commander Cody 52
Commander Gree 53
Commander Neyo 54
Count Dooku 55
Crab Droid 56
Darth Maul 57
Darth Vader 58
Death Star Gunner 59

Depa Billaba 60
Dewback 61
Dexter Jettster 62
Doctor Evazan 63
Droideka 64
Droopy McCool 65
Dwarf Spider Droid 66
Eeth Koth 67
Elan Sleazebaggano 68
EV-9D9 69
Even Piell 70
Figrin D'an 71
FX-series Med Droid 72
Gamorrean Guard 73
Garindan 74
General Cracken 75
General Grievous 76
General Madine 77
General Rieekan 78
General Veers 79
Geonosian Soldier 80
GH-7 Medical Droid 81
Grand Moff Tarkin 82
Greeata 83
Greedo 84
Hailfire Droid 85
Han Solo 86
Homing Spider Droid 87
Hoth Rebel Trooper 88

IG-88 89
Imperial Dignitary 90
Imperial Droids 91
Imperial Probot 92
Imperial Red Guard 93
Interrogator Droid 94
J'Quille 95
Jabba the Hutt 96
Jan Dodonna 97
Jango Fett 98
Jar Jar Binks 99
Jawa 100
Jocasta Nu 101
Ki-Adi-Mundi 102
Kit Fisto 103
Ko Sai 104
Lama Su 105
Lando Calrissian 106
Lobot 107
Logray 108
Luke Skywalker 109
Luminara Unduli 110
Lyn Me 111
Mace Windu 112
MagnaGuard 113
Malakili 114
Mas Amedda 115
Max Rebo 116
Moff Jerjerrod 117
Mon Mothma 118
Muftak 119
Mustafarian (Northern) 120
Mustafarian (Southern) 121
Naboo Guard 122
Nexu 123
Nien Nunb 124
Nute Gunray 125
Obi-Wan Kenobi 126
Octuptarra Droid 127
Oola 128

OOM-9 129
Opee Sea Killer 130
Oppo Rancisis 131
Owen Lars 132
Padmé Amidala 133
Palpatine 134
Passel Argente 135
Pau'an Warrior 136
Pilot Droid 137
Pit Droid 138
Plo Koon 139
Podracers 140
Poggle the Lesser 141
Polis Massan 142
Ponda Baba 143
Power Droid 144
Princess Leia 145
Queen Apailana 146
Qui-Gon Jinn 147
R2-D2 148
R4-G9 149
R4-P17 150
R5-D4 151
Rancor 152
Rappertunie 153
Rebel Trooper 154
Reek 155
Rune Haako 156
Rystáll 157
Sabé 158
Saelt-Marae 159
Saesee Tiin 160
Salacious Crumb 161
San Hill 162
Sando Aqua Monster 163
Sandtrooper 164
Sarlacc 165
Scout Trooper 166
Sebulba 167
Security Droid 168

Sei Taria 169
Shaak Ti 170
Shmi Skywalker 171
Shock Trooper 172
Shu Mai 173
Sio Bibble 174
Sly Moore 175
Snowtrooper 176
Space Slug 177
Stass Allie 178
Stormtrooper 179
Sun Fac 180
Super Battle Droid 181
Sy Snootles 182
Tarfful 183
Tauntaun 184
Teebo 185
Ten Numb 186
Tessek 187
TIE Fighter Pilot 188
Tion Medon 189
Tusken Raider 190
Ugnaught 191
Utai 192
Wampa 193
Wat Tambor 194
Watto 195
Wicket W. Warrick 196
X-wing Pilots 197
Yaddle 198
Yarael Poof 199
Yarna 200
Yoda 201
Yuzzum 202
Zam Wesell 203
Zett Jukassa 204
Zuckuss 205

Index 206

2-1B
SURGICAL DROID

2-1B MEDICAL AND SURGICAL DROIDS have been around since Republic times. One such unit is attached to the Rebel base on Hoth. It treats the injuries of many Rebel troops, including Luke Skywalker after a wampa attacks him.

A Republic-era 2-1B droid rebuilds Darth Vader's burned body.

Fine motion hand

Transparent shell over hydraulics

Hydraulic leg

Rebel Surgeon

2-1B is able to perform extremely precise operations that leave little or no scar. The droid's long experience with humans makes it a caring medic. Luke Skywalker is so impressed with 2-1B's skills, he requests that the droid treat him again after he loses his hand on Cloud City.

Surgical droids

in the 2-1B series are equipped with encyclopedic memory banks. They ensure that the droids give the best course of treatment in any medical situation.

Stabilizing foot

4-LOM

PROTOCOL DROID TURNED BOUNTY HUNTER

THIS HUMANOID DROID with an insect-like face used to be a sophisticated protocol droid made to resemble the species it served. 4-LOM was once assigned to a luxury liner, but it overwrote its own programming and began a life of crime as a bounty hunter.

After the Battle of Hoth, Vader hires 4-LOM and others to locate the *Millennium Falcon*.

Compound photoreceptors

Dangerous Duo

4-LOM often works in partnership with a bounty hunter named Zuckuss. The combination of 4-LOM's powers of deduction and analysis with Zuckuss's mystical intuition makes their collaboration successful and lucrative.

Blastech W-90 concussion rifle

4-LOM is a highly intelligent and determined droid, with an unexpected capacity for kindness. At one point, 4-LOM joins the Rebellion against the Empire. But it returns to its cold, criminal ways a short time later, serving Jabba the Hutt and other criminals.

DATA FILE

AFFILIATION: Bounty hunter
TYPE: LOM-series protocol droid
MANUFACTURER: Industrial Automaton
HEIGHT: 1.6 m (5 ft 2 in)
APPEARANCES: V
SEE ALSO: Zuckuss; Jabba the Hutt; Darth Vader

Battered black droid plating

8D8
JABBA'S DROID TORTURER

CRUEL **8D8** works in Jabba's palace on Tatooine as a droid torturer. His job is to ensure all Jabba's droids and slaves know their place.

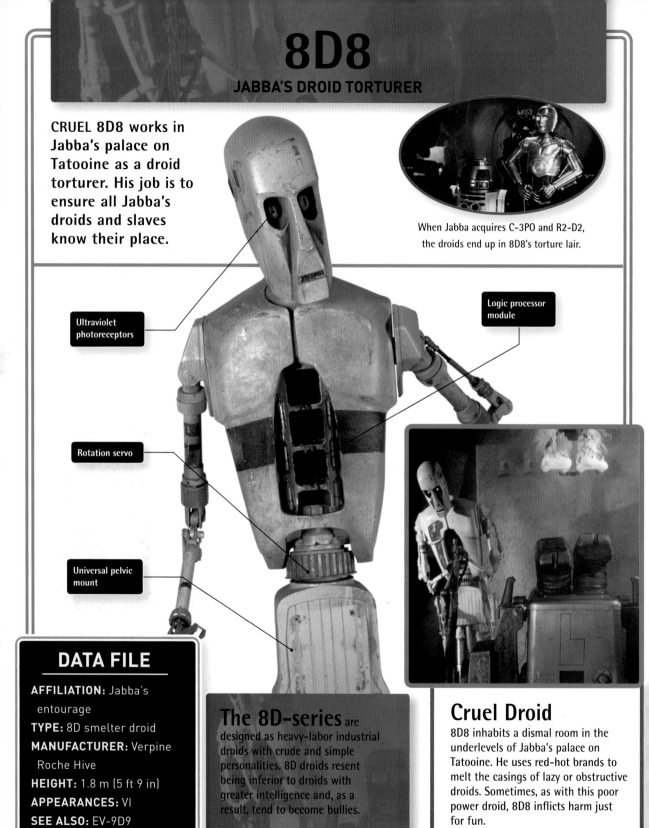

When Jabba acquires C-3PO and R2-D2, the droids end up in 8D8's torture lair.

Ultraviolet photoreceptors

Logic processor module

Rotation servo

Universal pelvic mount

DATA FILE

AFFILIATION: Jabba's entourage
TYPE: 8D smelter droid
MANUFACTURER: Verpine Roche Hive
HEIGHT: 1.8 m (5 ft 9 in)
APPEARANCES: VI
SEE ALSO: EV-9D9

The 8D-series are designed as heavy-labor industrial droids with crude and simple personalities. 8D droids resent being inferior to droids with greater intelligence and, as a result, tend to become bullies.

Cruel Droid

8D8 inhabits a dismal room in the underlevels of Jabba's palace on Tatooine. He uses red-hot brands to melt the casings of lazy or obstructive droids. Sometimes, as with this poor power droid, 8D8 inflicts harm just for fun.

AAYLA SECURA

TWI'LEK JEDI KNIGHT

CUNNING AAYLA SECURA is a Twi'lek Jedi Knight who relies on her athletic lightsaber skills to outwit opponents. As a Jedi General, Aayla leads a squad of clone troopers on many campaigns.

Secura's own clone troopers turn on her on Felucia.

Djem So attack stance

Lekku (head-tail)

Captured

At the Battle of Geonosis, Aayla Secura is among the circle of Jedi captured by Geonosian soldiers. Luckily, clone trooper reinforcements come to their rescue.

DATA FILE

AFFILIATION: Jedi
HOMEWORLD: Ryloth
SPECIES: Twi'lek
HEIGHT: 1.7 m (5 ft 7 in)
APPEARANCES: II, III, CW
SEE ALSO: Kit Fisto; Mace Windu; Yoda

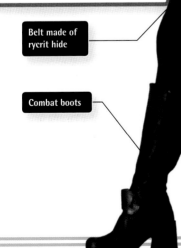

Belt made of rycrit hide

Combat boots

Fitted clothing allows complete freedom of movement

Aayla Secura is an intelligent, sometimes mischievous Jedi. Her Jedi teacher was a troubled Jedi named Quinlan Vos. They had many adventures together, including a brush with the dark side. Secura is also close to fellow Jedi Kit Fisto.

ACKLAY

GEONOSIS ARENA BEAST

CONDEMNED PRISONERS IN the Geonosis execution arenas face certain death by wild beast. Many of these creatures are caught and transported to Geonosis from their home planets far away. The ferocious acklay is one of these exotic beasts.

Acklays walk on long, clawed fingertips.

Razor-sharp teeth

Hardened skin-covered claw

DATA FILE

HOMEWORLD: Vendaxa
HEIGHT: 3.05 m (10 ft)
DIET: Carnivorous
HABITAT: Underwater, land
APPEARANCES: II
SEE ALSO: Nexu; reek; Obi-Wan Kenobi

The acklay's homeworld is a fertile planet named Vendaxa. They live underwater but emerge to the plains to hunt for creatures named lemnai.

Grappling hand

Stretchy stomach

Protective bony modules

Acklay Attack

Jedi Obi-Wan Kenobi uses a Geonosian picador's pike to defend himself against the savage acklay's onslaught.

ADI GALLIA

THOLOTHIAN JEDI MASTER

JEDI MASTER ADI GALLIA was born into a high-ranking diplomatic family stationed on Coruscant. Gallia is a Jedi High Council member and a noble General in the Clone Wars.

As a High Council member, Adi Gallia is respected for her powers of intuition.

Tholoth headdress

Adi Gallia is a valuable intelligence source to Senate leaders. She has many contacts throughout the Coruscant political machine, including her cousin, Stass Allie.

Lightsaber

Utility pouch

Jedi Temple

Gallia may be stationed at the Jedi Temple on Coruscant, but she is finely attuned to events further afield. Gallia is the first to warn the Senate of the Trade Federation's suspicious activity in the Naboo System.

DATA FILE

AFFILIATION: Jedi
HOMEWORLD: Coruscant
SPECIES: Tholothian
HEIGHT: 1.84 m (6 ft)
APPEARANCES: I, II, CW
SEE ALSO: Stass Allie; Even Piell; Chancellor Valorum; Bail Organa

Tall travel boots

Jedi robe

ADMIRAL ACKBAR
COMMANDER OF THE REBEL FLEET

ADMIRAL ACKBAR was born on the ocean world of Mon Calamari. When the Empire conquers his planet, Ackbar is presented as a slave to Grand Moff Tarkin. A rescue mission by the Rebels frees Ackbar and he convinces his people to join the Rebel Alliance.

Ackbar commands the Rebel fleet from his personal flagship, *Home One*.

DATA FILE

AFFILIATION: Rebel Alliance
HOMEWORLD: Mon Calamari
SPECIES: Mon Calamari
HEIGHT: 1.8 m (5 ft 11 in)
APPEARANCES: VI
SEE ALSO: Lando Calrissian;
Mon Mothma; General Madine

Command insignia

Mon Cal uniform jerkin

Waterproof skin

Utility belt

Home One

Ackbar's people contribute their giant Mon Cal star cruisers to the Alliance. *Home One* serves as a mobile command center after the Empire discovers and destroys all the Alliance's secret bases.

Moisture-retaining fabric

As commander of the Rebel fleet, Admiral Ackbar plans and leads the attack on the Empire's capital ships in the Battle of Endor.

ADMIRAL OZZEL

ADMIRAL OF THE *EXECUTOR*

KENDAL OZZEL IS THE COMMANDER of Darth Vader's gigantic flagship, the *Executor*. Under Ozzel's sometimes uncertain command, the *Executor* emerges from hyperspace too close to Hoth, alerting the Rebels to the Imperials' presence.

The *Executor* leads Darth Vader's personal fleet of Star Destroyers, known as Death Squadron.

Officer's disc

Imperial code cylinder

Rank insignia plaque

Belt buckle contains secret data-storage compartment

Durasteel-toed boots

Deadly Blunders

Vader's view of Ozzel is that he is "as clumsy as he is stupid." After a series of blunders—first, doubting evidence of life on Hoth, then the failed attempt to surprise the Rebels—Vader telekinetically executes Ozzel with the Force and promotes Captain Piett to Admiral in Ozzel's place.

Kendal Ozzel serves in the Republic Navy during the Clone Wars and soon works his way up the military ladder. Ozzel is ambitious but displays poor judgment and ineffective tactical thinking, which he attempts to mask with his authoritarian persona.

DATA FILE

AFFILIATION: Empire

HOMEWORLD: Carida

SPECIES: Human

HEIGHT: 1.7 m (5 ft 7 in)

APPEARANCES: V

SEE ALSO: Admiral Piett; General Veers; Darth Vader

ADMIRAL PIETT
COMMANDER OF THE *EXECUTOR*

PIETT IS A LOYAL IMPERIAL captain on Darth Vader's flagship, the *Executor*. After Vader Force-chokes Admiral Ozzel to death for incompetence, Piett is instantly promoted to Admiral of the fleet. Piett loses his life when a Rebel A-wing crashes through the bridge of the *Executor*.

An A-wing kills the *Executor*'s bridge crew and causes the ship to crash.

Imperial officer's disc

Imperial code cylinder

Risky Strategy

Vader's officers must submit entirely to the Dark Lord's iron will. When Vader insists that Piett makes a risky pursuit of the *Millennium Falcon* into an asteroid field, Piett nervously does Vader's bidding, aware that errors could lead to his death.

DATA FILE

AFFILIATION: Empire
HOMEWORLD: Axxila
SPECIES: Human
HEIGHT: 1.65 m (5 ft 5 in)
APPEARANCES: V, VI
SEE ALSO: Admiral Ozzel;
  Darth Vader

Unlike most Imperial officers, who come from the prestigious Inner Core worlds, Firmus Piett's origins are in the Outer Rim. He is known for his quick-thinking, as well as his ability to shift blame for mistakes he has made.

AGEN KOLAR

ZABRAK JEDI MASTER

AGEN KOLAR is a master swordsmith who joins the 200 Jedi Knights that battle the Separatist army on Geonosis. Mace Windu has a high opinion of Kolar's combat skills, and enlists him in a desperate attempt to arrest Supreme Chancellor Palpatine.

Agen Kolar's renowned lightsaber skills are put to use on Geonosis.

Horns regenerate over time

Lightsaber uses duel crystals to create green or blue energy blades

Two-handed ready stance

Hooded robe often removed in combat

Skillful Sith

Even the celebrated sword skills of Agen Kolar cannot match the speed and unsparing power of a Sith Lord such as Darth Sidious.

Agen Kolar is a Zabrak, as is fellow Jedi Eeth Koth. The Zabrak species is identified by its head horns. Known to strike first and ask questions later, Kolar is also a valuable member of the Jedi High Council.

DATA FILE

AFFILIATION: Jedi
HOMEWORLD: Coruscant
SPECIES: Zabrak
HEIGHT: 1.7 m (5 ft 5 in)
APPEARANCES: II, III
SEE ALSO: Mace Windu; Saesee Tiin; Kit Fisto

ANAKIN SKYWALKER
LEGENDARY JEDI KNIGHT

ANAKIN SKYWALKER'S RISE to power is astonishing. In a few short years he goes from being a slave on Tatooine to becoming one of the most powerful Jedi ever. But Anakin's thirst for power leads him to the dark side of the Force, with tragic consequences for the galaxy.

Young Anakin's keen perception and unnaturally fast reflexes show his great Force potential.

Gauntlet covers mechno-hand (which replaces hand sliced off by Count Dooku)

Jedi utility belt

Close Bond
Anakin's bond with his teacher, Obi-Wan Kenobi, is strong. They make a dynamic team in the Clone Wars, where Anakin proves to be a great leader. Yet Anakin is troubled by feelings of anger and mistrust.

DATA FILE

AFFILIATION: Jedi
HOMEWORLD: Tatooine
SPECIES: Human
HEIGHT: 1.85 m (6 ft 1 in)
APPEARANCES: I, II, III, VI, CW
SEE ALSO: Qui-Gon Jinn; Obi-Wan Kenobi; Padmé Amidala

In the Clone Wars,
Anakin loses his faith in the Jedi to restore peace and harmony to the galaxy. He also feels great anger at the tragic death of his mother and fears that the same fate may befall Padmé Amidala (who is secretly his wife). Finally, Anakin is persuaded that only the dark side can give him the power to prevent death.

AT-AT PILOT
IMPERIAL WALKER OPERATORS

ONLY THE STRONGEST Imperial soldiers are put forward for training to become pilots of the terrifying All Terrain Armored Transport (AT-AT) walkers. AT-AT pilots, who generally work in pairs, believe themselves all-powerful.

The pilots sit in the cockpit in the AT-AT's head, operating driving and firing controls.

Reinforced helmet

Life support pack

Driving gauntlet

Insulated jumpsuit

Walking Terror
The giant AT-AT walkers march relentlessly across uneven battlegrounds, using their mighty laser cannons to create destruction and terror to enemy forces below.

AT-ATs are not climate controlled, so pilots wear special insulated suits on frozen planets such as Hoth. The suits protect the wearer if the walker's pressurized cockpit is smashed open in hostile environments.

DATA FILE

AFFILIATION: Empire
SPECIES: Human
AVERAGE HEIGHT:
  1.83 m (6 ft)
STANDARD EQUIPMENT:
  Blaster pistol; thermal detonators; grenades
APPEARANCES: V
SEE ALSO: AT-ST pilot; General Veers

AT-ST PILOT

IMPERIAL SCOUT WALKER CREW

TWO-LEGGED AT-ST (All Terrain Scout Transport) walkers march into battle, spraying blaster bolts at enemy troops. Each walker houses two pilots, trained to develop superior skills of balance and agility.

Two pilots keep the AT-ST walker moving at speed through uneven terrain.

DATA FILE

AFFILIATION: Empire
SPECIES: Human
STANDARD EQUIPMENT:
  Blasters; grenades;
  thermal detonators;
  emergency flares; comlink
APPEARANCES: VI
SEE ALSO: AT-AT pilot;
Chewbacca

Fire-resistant gauntlet

Jumpsuit

Leather boots

On the Hunt

AT-ST walkers are used on reconnaissance and anti-personnel hunting missions. They are not invulnerable to attack, as Chewbacca demonstrates when he forces his way inside a walker through the roof.

AT-ST pilots wear open-face helmets, blast goggles, and basic armor plating underneath their jumpsuits. In the Battle of Endor, AT-ST walkers are deployed against the Rebels. Many are lost to surprise attacks by Ewoks.

AURRA SING

VICIOUS BOUNTY HUNTER

AURRA SING IS A RUTHLESS bounty hunter. Rumor has it that Sing trained as a Jedi as a youth, but her aggressive nature held her back and she left the Jedi Order. In the Clone Wars, she is hired to attempt to assassinate Senator Padmé Amidala.

During the Clone Wars, Aurra guides the recently orphaned Boba Fett.

Aurra Sing was born
in the polluted urban sprawl of Nar Shaddaa. She never knew her father and her mother was too poor to raise her. Sing became a cold-blooded killer. She is willing to use any means necessary to locate her prey. She has sensor implants and has a wide assortment of weapons in her private arsenal, including lightsabers and a sniper's projectile rifle.

Tracker utility vest

Short-range pistol

Long fingers to draw blood

High Alert
On the trail of Jedi Knights on Tatooine, Aurra Sing is a spectator at the Podrace that will earn young Anakin Skywalker his freedom.

Long-range projectile rifle

DATA FILE

AFFILIATION: Bounty hunter
HOMEWORLD: Nar Shaddaa
SPECIES: Near-human
HEIGHT: 1.83 m (6 ft)
APPEARANCES: I, CW
SEE ALSO: Bossk; Padmé Amidala; Boba Fett

A-WING PILOT

ELITE REBEL PILOTS

A-WINGS ARE small, super-fast starfighters and A-wing pilots are some of the most talented fliers in the Rebel Alliance. These pilots play a pivotal role at the Battle of Endor when they destroy Vader's ship, the *Executor*.

Rebel pilot Arvel Crynyd pilots his damaged A-wing into the bridge of the *Executor*.

DATA FILE

AFFILIATION:
Rebel Alliance
SQUADRON NAME:
Green Group
SQUADRON LEADER:
Arvel Crynyd
APPEARANCES: VI
SEE ALSO: Admiral Ackbar;
Lando Calrissian

Flak vest

Pressurized g-suit

Data cylinders

Gear harness

Arvel Crynyd leads the
A-wing Green Group during the Battle of Endor. Hit by fire from the *Executor* during a bombing raid, Crynyd skillfully pilots his crippled ship through the unshielded bridge of Vader's ship, instantly killing the entire bridge crew.

Capable Ships

Only the very best Rebel pilots can fly the powerful A-wings. Designed before the Battle of Endor as an escort ship, the A-wing's incredible speed and maneuverability makes it a deadly strike craft. They also use concealed sensors to gather information on Imperial ships.

B'OMARR MONK

MYSTERIOUS DISEMBODIED MONKS

THE B'OMARR MONKS ARE the original inhabitants of Jabba the Hutt's palace on Tatooine. When these mysterious monks reach the highest state of enlightenment, their living brains are surgically removed from their bodies and placed in special jars. These jars are carried around on mechanical legs.

The B'omarr monks built the monastery that Jabba the Hutt took as his palace on Tatooine.

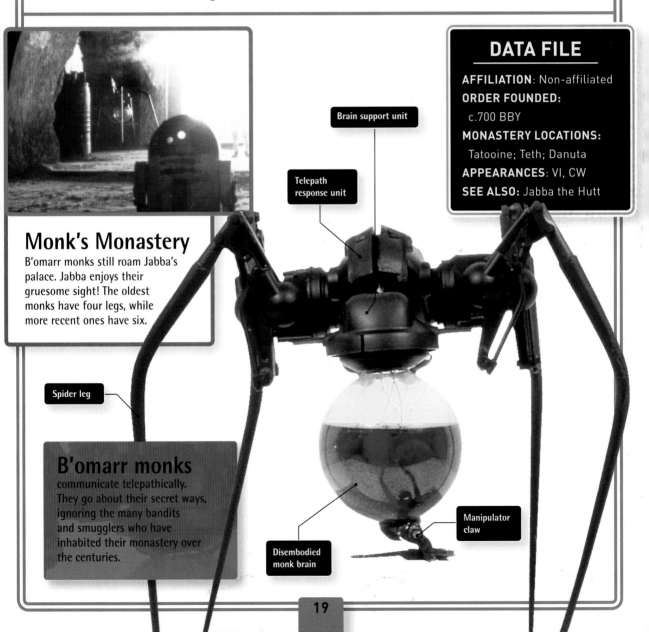

Brain support unit

Telepath response unit

Monk's Monastery

B'omarr monks still roam Jabba's palace. Jabba enjoys their gruesome sight! The oldest monks have four legs, while more recent ones have six.

Spider leg

B'omarr monks

communicate telepathically. They go about their secret ways, ignoring the many bandits and smugglers who have inhabited their monastery over the centuries.

Disembodied monk brain

Manipulator claw

BAIL ORGANA
VICEROY OF ALDERAAN

BAIL ORGANA IS the Senator for Alderaan. He watches, horrified, as the Galactic Republic becomes a dictatorship under Palpatine. Bail is one of the founders, with Mon Mothma, of the Rebellion against Emperor Palpatine.

Bail and his wife, Breha, adopt Leia Amidala Skywalker.

DATA FILE

AFFILIATION: Republic/ Rebel Alliance
HOMEWORLD: Alderaan
SPECIES: Human
HEIGHT: 1.91 m (6 ft 3 in)
APPEARANCES: II, III, CW
SEE ALSO: Princess Leia; Mon Mothma

Narrow Escape

Bail is the first civilian to arrive at the Jedi Temple after the massacres carried out by Anakin and his legion of clone troopers. Bail narrowly escapes the Temple with his own life.

Forearm plate

Target blaster

Action boots

Alderaan belt

Alderaanian cloak

Organa remains loyal to the Republic and the Jedi Order to the end. In Imperial times, it is Bail who responds to the threat of the Death Star by sending his adopted daughter, Leia, on a mission to locate Obi-Wan Kenobi in order to recruit him to the Alliance.

BANTHA
TATOOINE BEASTS OF BURDEN

FOR FARMERS AND SETTLERS on Tatooine, a Tusken Raider riding a bantha is a dreaded sight. Tusken Raiders form close bonds with these huge beasts, and use them to carry riders and transport belongings. They even make banthas members of their clans.

Herds of banthas wander the dunes and wastes, led by a dominant female.

Spiral horn

Tusken Rider
Tusken Raiders ride banthas in single file to hide their numbers. Tuskens are bonded with a single bantha from a young age.

Both male
and female banthas grow spiral horns, which grow at a rate of a knob a year. Banthas can go without food or water for several weeks, making them suited to life in harsh environments like Tatooine.

Three-toed hoof

Sack for food and supplies

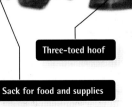

DATA FILE

HABITAT: Various
HEIGHT: 2.5 m (8 ft 2 in)
DIET: Herbivorous
LIFESPAN: 80–100 years
APPEARANCES: I, II, IV, VI, CW
SEE ALSO: Tusken Raider

BARON PAPANOIDA

INFLUENTIAL PANTORAN TRADE GUILD BARON

BARON PAPANOIDA LIVES on Coruscant where he funds an influential entertainment empire. He is known to be a critic of Palpatine, although much of his life is shrouded in secrecy and it is rumored that he may be a double agent.

Papanoida meets with his daughter, Chi Eekway, at the opera house.

Ceremonial shoulder cord

Pantoran emblem

Stripes on sleeve indicate rank

Dress gloves

Networks

Papanoida meets with many important Senators and others in his private box at the Galaxies Opera House. He feeds them information from his network of informants.

The Baron

becomes Chairman of the Pantoran Assembly after the death of Chairman Chi Cho on the ice moon, Orto Plutonia. He is embroiled in the Clone Wars when the Trade Federation kidnaps his two daughters, Che Amanwe and Chi Eekway. With his son, Ion, Papanoida engages some of the kidnappers in Mos Eisley.

DATA FILE

AFFILIATION: Republic
HOMEWORLD: Pantora
SPECIES: Pantoran
HEIGHT: 1.7 m (5 ft 6 in)
APPEARANCES: III, CW
SEE ALSO: Chi Eekway Papanoida; Palpatine

BARRISS OFFEE
MIRIALAN JEDI KNIGHT AND GENERAL

JEDI KNIGHT BARRISS OFFEE is thoughtful, daring, and selfless. She is the Padawan learner of Jedi Master Luminara Unduli, to whom she is completely loyal. Together these two Jedi make a formidable pairing.

Offee practices a style of lightsaber fighting known as Soresu.

Mirialan tattoos

Two-handed grip for control

Belt contains secret compartments

DATA FILE

AFFILIATION: Jedi
HOMEWORLD: Mirial
SPECIES: Mirialan
HEIGHT: 1.66 m (5 ft 5 in)
APPEARANCES: II, CW
SEE ALSO: Luminara Unduli; Shaak Ti

Powerful Team

Offee specializes in tandem fighting and she uses the Force to keep her actions perfectly in sync with her partner Unduli. The team of Unduli and Offee is more powerful than the sum of its parts.

Hooded robe

Like Luminara

Unduli, Barriss Offee is a Mirialan, a yellow-green skinned species. Mirialan are known for tattoos on their faces and hands, which indicate accomplishments.

BATTLE DROID
MECHANICAL DROID SOLDIERS

BATTLE DROIDS are the ground troops of the Separatist army: fearless, emotionless, and ready to do their masters' bidding. Battle droids are designed to resemble their Geonosian creators.

Battle droids are first deployed against the peaceful people of Naboo.

Arm extension piston

Simple vocoder

Battle droids

are intended to win by strength of numbers rather than by individual ability. The droids are mass-produced and unable to think independently. A computer on board a Trade Federation ship feeds them all their mission commands.

E-5 blaster rifle

Limbs resemble Neimoidian skeletons

DATA FILE

AFFILIATION: Separatist
TYPE: B1 battle droid
MANUFACTURER: Baktoid Armor Workshop
HEIGHT: 1.91 m (6 ft 3 in)
APPEARANCES: I, II, III, CW
SEE ALSO: Droideka; super battle droid

Folding knee joint

STAPs

Battle droid scouts and snipers are swept through the air on armed Single Trooper Aerial Platforms, or STAPs. These repulsorlift vehicles can thread through dense forests that would be inaccessible to larger vehicles.

BERU LARS

LUKE SKYWALKER'S GUARDIAN

BERU LARS'S family has been made up of moisture farmers for three generations. At the end of the Clone Wars, Obi-Wan Kenobi asks Beru and her husband, Owen, to raise Luke Skywalker, while he lives nearby to watch over the boy.

Beru and Owen agree to adopt Luke to protect him from the evil of the Empire.

Simple hairstyle

DATA FILE

AFFILIATION: Republic
HOMEWORLD: Tatooine
SPECIES: Human
HEIGHT: 1.65 m (5 ft 5 in)
APPEARANCES: II, III, IV
SEE ALSO: Owen Lars;
Luke Skywalker

Desert tunic

Protector

As Luke becomes a young adult, Beru understands his desire to leave home and join the Imperial Academy. But she also knows the truth about Luke's father, and respects Owen's desire to protect Luke from following in Anakin's footsteps.

Beru Lars is

hard-working and self-reliant. She is well-equipped to deal with most of the dangers encountered in the Tatooine desert. However, nothing can prepare Beru for the group of Imperial stormtroopers that come in search of the two renegade droids carrying stolen Death Star plans.

Rough clothing made in Anchorhead

Desert boots

BIB FORTUNA
JABBA'S TWI'LEK MAJOR-DOMO

THE SINISTER BIB FORTUNA oversees the day-to-day affairs of Jabba the Hutt's desert palace and his estate in Mos Eisley. Before working with Jabba, Bib Fortuna became rich as a slave trader of his own people, the Twi'leks.

Fortuna hovers near Jabba's ear, whispering advice. Secretly, he plots to kill Jabba!

Bib Fortuna is a powerful and dreaded individual in Jabba's entourage. Whether you are a friend or a foe, Fortuna will use underhand means against you in order to maintain his control within the organization.

Tricked

Bib Fortuna has been Jabba's major-domo (head of staff) for many decades. But when two droids arrive unexpectedly to bargain for Han Solo's life, Fortuna unwittingly kickstarts a chain of events that leads to the downfall of the notorious Hutt gangster.

Lekku (head-tail; one of two)

Traditional Ryloth robe

Silver bracelet

Soft-soled shoes for silent creeping

DATA FILE

AFFILIATION: Jabba's entourage
HOMEWORLD: Ryloth
SPECIES: Twi'lek
HEIGHT: 1.8 m (5 ft 11 in)
APPEARANCES: I, VI, CW
SEE ALSO: Jabba the Hutt

BOBA FETT

THE BEST BOUNTY HUNTER IN THE GALAXY

COOL AND CALCULATING, Boba Fett is a legendary bounty hunter. He is paid to track down and, often, kill targeted individuals. Over the years, Fett has developed a code of honor, and only accepts missions which meet this harsh sense of justice.

Working for Darth Vader, Fett captures Han Solo and loads his carbon-frozen body into *Slave I*.

Multifunction helmet

EE-3 blaster rifle

Reinforced flight suit

Utility belt

DATA FILE

AFFILIATION: Bounty hunter

HOMEWORLD: Kamino

SPECIES: Human

HEIGHT: 1.83 m (6 ft)

APPEARANCES: II, IV, V, VI, CW

SEE ALSO: Jango Fett; Darth Vader; Han Solo; Jabba the Hutt

Like Father, Like Son

Boba Fett is an exact genetic clone of Jango Fett, who brings Boba up as a son. Boba witnesses Jango's death at the Battle of Geonosis and swears revenge against the Jedi who killed him. In time, he inherits Jango Fett's Mandalorian battle armor and his ship, *Slave I*.

Boba Fett's talent and skill, combined with an arsenal of exotic weapons, has brought in many "impossible" bounties. He is notorious for completely disintegrating those whom he has been hired to track down.

BOGA

OBI-WAN KENOBI'S MOUNT ON UTAPAU

BOGA IS A DOMESTICATED LIZARD called a varactyl. On Utapau, Obi-Wan Kenobi rides Boga across the planet's hazardous sinkholes and sheer cliff faces in search of General Grievous. Boga is well-trained and highly responsive to the Jedi's command.

Boga and Kenobi plunge down a sinkhole after turncoat clones unleash a hail of blaster fire.

Varactyls have powerful limbs and clawed feet, which makes them fast runners and excellent climbers. On Utapau, they are coralled by wranglers and used as transports.

Spines for defense

DATA FILE

HOMEWORLD: Utapau
LENGTH:
15 m (49 ft 3 in)
DIET: Herbivorous
HABITAT: Utapaun
sinkholes
APPEARANCES:
III
SEE ALSO:
Utai

Crest present in both male and female

Five-clawed feet provide excellent purchase

Swift Boga

Boga, with Obi-Wan Kenobi in the saddle, keeps pace with General Grievous on his Wheel Bike. After many twists and turns, with Boga's help, Obi-Wan confronts and destroys the General.

BOSS NASS

GUNGAN LEADER

BOSS NASS IS THE stern, old-fashioned ruler of Otoh Gunga, the largest of the Gungan underwater cities on Naboo. He speaks Galactic Basic (the most widely used language in the galaxy) with a strong accent.

The Gungan High Council has the power to summon the Gungan Grand Army.

Crown of rulership

Epaulets of military authority

Four-fingered hand

Teamwork

When his planet is faced with invasion, Boss Nass puts aside his prejudice against the Naboo. He receives Queen Amidala when she humbly asks him for help. Boss Nass realizes that his people must work together with the Naboo or die, and a new friendship is forged between the two cultures.

DATA FILE

AFFILIATION: Republic
HOMEWORLD: Naboo
SPECIES: Gungan
HEIGHT: 2.06 m (6 ft 9 in)
APPEARANCES: I, III
SEE ALSO: Padmé Amidala; Jar Jar Binks

Long coat with golden clasp

Boss Nass sits on the Gungan High Council. He is a fair but stubborn ruler. He particularly resents the Naboo's belief that the Gungans are primitive simply because Gungans prefer to use traditional crafts and technologies.

Gungan sandals

BOSSK

TRANDOSHAN BOUNTY HUNTER

THE TOUGH AND RESILIENT Bossk is a reptilian Trandoshan bounty hunter. He used to track runaway slaves. Now he claims bounties for the Empire, and has a count of 12 captives so far.

Bossk and other bounty hunters frequently visit Jabba the Hutt, seeking their next job.

Eyes can see in infrared range

Flak vest

Blaster rifle

Lost fingers, skin, and even limbs can regrow until adulthood

Tough Trandoshan

Fond of skinning his captives when possible, Bossk is as vile and mean as bounty hunters get. He is one of the six bounty hunters Darth Vader enlists to track down and capture the *Millennium Falcon*.

DATA FILE

AFFILIATION: Bounty hunter
HOMEWORLD: Trandosha
SPECIES: Trandoshan
HEIGHT: 1.9 m (6 ft 3 in)
APPEARANCES: V, VI, CW
SEE ALSO: Aurra Sing;
  Boba Fett; Darth Vader

Bossk began his career doing a form of bounty hunting that few other species would risk: hunting Wookiees. Later, he hunts other species. During the Clone Wars, Bossk teams up with Aurra Sing, young Boba Fett, and a Klatooinian bounty hunter named Castas.

BOUSHH
PRINCESS LEIA IN DISGUISE

THE GALAXY CONTAINS many bizarre creatures acting as bounty hunters (or claiming to be). Princess Leia adopts a convincing identity as a Ubese tracker, Boushh, to gain entry to Jabba's palace. Only Jabba suspects her identity.

Leia, in disguise as Boushh, prepares to release Han Solo from frozen captivity.

Speech scrambler

Projectile detonator

Glove spikes

Ammo pouch

DATA FILE

AFFILIATION: Bounty hunter
HOMEWORLD: Uba IV
SPECIES: Ubese
HEIGHT: 1.5 m (5 ft)
APPEARANCES: VI
SEE ALSO: Princess Leia; Chewbacca; Jabba the Hutt

Shata leather pants

Boushh's Undoing

At Jabba's palace, Chewbacca pretends to be Boushh's captive while Boushh pulls out a thermal detonator. The real Boushh worked for many paymasters, but his downfall came when he accepted work from—and then tried to blackmail—the Black Sun crime syndicate.

Boushh's survival clothing and optically enhanced helmet fit Leia perfectly. She has used the disguise once before, on a mission to meet with Xizor, the leader of the powerful criminal organization Black Sun.

Traditional Ubese boots

31

BULTAR SWAN

JEDI KNIGHT AND GENERAL

JEDI KNIGHT BULTAR Swan is a survivor of the Great Jedi Purge, in which clone troops kill most of her fellow Jedi. Afterward, she and seven other Jedi survivors face Darth Vader. Swan slices off Vader's sword arm, but refuses to deal the final blow to an unarmed opponent.

Fellow Jedi Koffi Arana takes Swan's life in order to strike Vader, but is himself killed in the attempt.

Swan served as a Jedi General during the Clone Wars. Her lightsaber skills are flawless. She draws in her opponents by making very few physical movements. Then she strikes suddenly. Bultar's attack appears as a single blaze of motion, but is in fact a highly complex sequence of moves.

Two-handed grip for control

Utility belt

Synthetic leather surcoat

DATA FILE

AFFILIATION: Jedi

HOMEWORLD: Kuat

SPECIES: Human

HEIGHT: 1.68 m (5 ft 6 in)

APPEARANCES: II

SEE ALSO: Plo Koon

Apprentice

Swan was apprenticed to Jedi Master and High Council member Micah Giiett. After Giiett's death, his close friend Master Plo Koon takes over Swan's training.

BUZZ DROID

SEPARATIST SABOTAGE DROID

BUZZ DROIDS ARE small droids used by the Separatist armies. Swarms of buzz droids attack enemy ships, dodging their way through defenses with their maneuvering thrusters. They use their manipulator arms and cutting tools to inflict as much damage as possible.

Feisty R2-D2 targets a buzz droid's weak point: its primary photoreceptor eye.

Shock-absorbing outer hull

Communications antenna

Droid brain

Under Attack

In the Battle of Coruscant, buzz droids attack Obi-Wan's starfighter and destroy his astromech droid, R4-P17.

Circular saw

Primary photoreceptor

Separatist droid tri-fighters and vulture droid starfighters fire jet-powered discord missiles at enemy targets. Each discord missile contains up to seven buzz droids, enclosed in spherical casings, which split open to reveal the droid inside.

Targeting rangefinder

DATA FILE

AFFILIATION: Separatist
TYPE: Sabotage droid
MANUFACTURER:
Colicoid Creation Nest
WIDTH: 25 cm (10 in)
APPEARANCES: III
SEE ALSO: Obi-Wan Kenobi; R2-D2

C-3PO
GOLDEN PROTOCOL DROID

C-3PO IS PROGRAMMED to assist in matters of etiquette and translation. Thrown into a world of adventure, he is often overwhelmed by the action around him. But he forms a capable team when partnered with the resourceful R2-D2.

Anakin Skywalker built the working skeleton of C-3PO from scrap parts.

Vocabulator

Primary power couplet outlet

DATA FILE

AFFILIATION: Droid
TYPE: Protocol droid
MANUFACTURER: Cybot Galactica
HEIGHT: 1.67 m (5 ft 6 in)
APPEARANCES: I—VI, CW
SEE ALSO: R2-D2; Anakin Skywalker; Luke Skywalker

Golden God

Despite his fear of excitement, C-3PO has led an adventurous life, often losing limbs or bits of circuitry along the way (though he is easily repaired). On Endor, a tribe of Ewoks worships C-3PO as a "golden god," which leads the Ewoks to support the Rebels and play a decisive role in defeating the Empire for good.

C-3PO first worked for Anakin Skywalker and his mother, Shmi. Anakin then gave C-3PO to Senator Padmé Amidala as a wedding gift. After Padmé's death, C-3PO was assigned to Bail Organa, until Darth Vader captured the *Tantive IV*. C-3PO escaped to Tatooine and was sold to Luke Skywalker.

Reinforced knee joint

Bronzium finish polished to a dazzling sheen

CAPTAIN ANTILLES

CAPTAIN OF THE *TANTIVE IV*

CAPTAIN RAYMUS ANTILLES is commander of Bail Organa's fleet of diplomatic cruisers. Under the Empire, Antilles becomes a Rebel and serves as captain of the *Tantive IV* under Organa's adopted daughter, Leia Organa.

The Alderaan royal family owns the diplomatic cruiser *Tantive IV*.

DATA FILE

AFFILIATION: Republic/ Rebel Alliance
HOMEWORLD: Alderaan
SPECIES: Human
HEIGHT: 1.88 m (6 ft 2 in)
APPEARANCES: III, IV
SEE ALSO: Bail Organa; Princess Leia

Stranglehold

In the battle over Tatooine, Darth Vader boards the *Tantive IV* and demands that Antilles surrenders the stolen Death Star plans. When he refuses, Vader destroys him.

Wrist guard

Target blaster

Cape of Alderaanian nobility

Captain Antilles is a highly capable pilot. He has taken part in many daring missions for the Rebels, and has had notable success breaking through Imperial blockades.

Flight boots

CAPTAIN NEEDA

COMMANDER OF THE *AVENGER*

CAPTAIN NEEDA IS COMMANDER of the Imperial Star Destroyer *Avenger*, which takes part in the search for the Rebels' hidden bases. Needa follows the *Falcon* into an asteroid field and back out, but then loses the ship completely.

Needa fails to see that the *Falcon* "disappeared" by clinging to the side of his Star Destroyer.

Standard-issue officer's gloves

Belt buckle with data storage

Imperial officer's tunic

No Mercy

When Needa loses sight of the *Falcon*, he apologizes to Vader, accepting full responsibility. Vader accepts Needa's apology—then Force-strangles him.

DATA FILE

AFFILIATION: Empire
HOMEWORLD: Coruscant
SPECIES: Human
HEIGHT: 1.75 m (5 ft 9 in)
APPEARANCES: V
SEE ALSO: Darth Vader; Admiral Ozzel

Lorth Needa is a dependable and ruthless officer who served the Galactic Republic in the Clone Wars during the Battle of Coruscant, when General Grievous "kidnapped" Chancellor Palpatine. Now an Imperial officer, Needa fails to live up to Vader's exacting standards.

CAPTAIN PANAKA

NABOO HEAD OF SECURITY

AS HEAD OF SECURITY for Queen Amidala on Naboo, Captain Panaka oversees every branch of the volunteer Royal Naboo Security Forces. During the invasion of Naboo, Panaka sees the dangerous state of affairs in the galaxy and argues for stronger security measures.

After Queen Amidala's abdication, Panaka serves Queen Jamillia.

Leather jerkin

Utility belt

High officer headgear

Stripes on coat indicate rank

Royal Responsibility

Panaka is responsible for Queen Amidala's safety, accompanying her during the escape from Naboo. When the Queen returns to Naboo to reclaim her throne, Panaka is by her side, offering cover fire during the infiltration of the Palace.

DATA FILE

AFFILIATION: Republic
HOMEWORLD: Naboo
SPECIES: Human
HEIGHT: 1.83 m (6 ft)
APPEARANCES: I
SEE ALSO: Padmé Amidala

Captain Panaka

gained combat experience in a Republic Special Task Force, fighting against space pilots in the sector containing the Naboo system.

CAPTAIN TYPHO
SENATOR AMIDALA'S HEAD OF SECURITY

CAPTAIN TYPHO is well-respected for his loyalty. His uncle, Captain Panaka, was head of security for Padmé Amidala when she was Queen of Naboo. Now Typho oversees security for Padmé in her role as Senator for Naboo.

Captain Typho is by Amidala's side on many missions throughout the Clone Wars.

Eye lost during battle of Naboo

Synthetic leather gauntlets

Naboo blaster

Security uniform

A Dangerous World

Captain Typho accompanies Senator Amidala to Coruscant, where an assassination attempt kills seven in his command, including Padmé's handmaiden Cordé (disguised as Padmé). Typho soon realizes that even his strict security measures may not be enough in the new, dangerous world of the Clone Wars.

At the time of the Battle of Naboo, Typho was a Junior Palace Guard. Despite his young age, Typho played a brave part in the conflict, losing his eye in the line of duty. Captain Typho is given his Senatorial post because of his loyalty and his ties to Panaka.

DATA FILE

AFFILIATION: Republic
HOMEWORLD: Naboo
SPECIES: Human
HEIGHT: 1.85 m (6 ft 1 in)
APPEARANCES: II, III, CW
SEE ALSO: Padmé Amidala; Captain Panaka

CHANCELLOR VALORUM
HEAD OF THE REPUBLIC BEFORE PALPATINE

BEFORE PALPATINE BECOMES Supreme Chancellor, Finis Valorum holds the highest position in the Galactic Senate. He rules the Republic when Trade Federation warships blockade the peaceful planet of Naboo. Padmé Amidala blames Valorum personally.

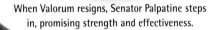

When Valorum resigns, Senator Palpatine steps in, promising strength and effectiveness.

Ornate overcloak

Blue band symbolic of Supreme Chancellor

Weak Leader

While Naboo suffers, the Senate debates its options, but does not act. The Speaker, Mas Amedda (secretly working for Palpatine), knows that this indecision will make Valorum look weak and ineffective.

DATA FILE

AFFILIATION: Republic
HOMEWORLD: Coruscant
SPECIES: Human
HEIGHT: 1.7 m (5 ft 7 in)
APPEARANCES: I
SEE ALSO: Palpatine; Padmé Amidala; Mas Amedda

Valorum comes from a family of politicians. All his life, he has been preparing for the office of Supreme Chancellor. This is a man who enjoys the privileges of a head of state. However, this attitude does not endear him to ordinary voters.

Veda cloth robe

CHEWBACCA

WOOKIEE WARRIOR, PILOT, AND REBEL

CHEWBACCA is a Wookiee warrior. In the Clone Wars, he serves under Wookiee leader Tarfful to defend his planet. After the Empire sells Chewbacca into slavery, Han Solo rescues him and they become best friends.

The Wookiees fight hard, but all is lost when Order 66 is activated.

DATA FILE

AFFILIATION: Republic/ Rebel Alliance
HOMEWORLD: Kashyyyk
SPECIES: Wookiee
HEIGHT: 2.28 m (7 ft 6 in)
APPEARANCES: III, IV, V, VI, CW
SEE ALSO: Han Solo; Tarfful

Ammunition bandolier

Bowcaster

Water-shedding hair

Powerful thighs

Wookiee Mechanic

The great Wookiee uses his mechanical abilities to keep Solo's spaceship flying. Later, he will employ these skills to completely reconstruct C-3PO after the poor droid is blasted apart on Cloud City.

Chewbacca serves as Han Solo's fiercely loyal copilot and trusty fellow adventurer. He enjoys the thrilling action that Solo gets them into, but sometimes tries to act as a check on his partner's willfulness.

CHI EEKWAY PAPANOIDA

PANTORAN SENATOR

CHI EEKWAY PAPANOIDA is a young Senator from Pantora, the moon of Orto Plutonia. Along with her father, Baron Papanoida, Chi is among the inner circle that advises Supreme Chancellor Palpatine during the Clone Wars.

Chi Eekway and Padmé Amidala share concerns over Palpatine's use of emergency powers.

Blue skin can withstand low temperatures

DATA FILE

AFFILIATION: Republic
HOMEWORLD: Pantora
SPECIES: Pantoran
HEIGHT: 1.65 m (5 ft 5 in)
APPEARANCES: III, CW
SEE ALSO: Baron
  Papanoida; Palpatine

Wroonian healing stones

Ornate overcloak

Loyalists

Chi Eekway is a member of the Loyalist committee that Supreme Chancellor Palpatine sets up to advise him during the Clone Wars. However, it is likely that the committee is really a means for Palpatine to keep a close eye on politicians whom he considers to be potential enemies.

Chi Eekway is

strong and patient. She uses her youth and powers of empathy to represent her independent home world Pantora. During the Clone Wars, Chi and her sister are kidnapped in a failed attempt to sway Pantora into joining the Confederacy.

41

CHIEF CHIRPA

EWOK LEADER

WISE CHIEF CHIRPA has led the Bright Tree tribe on the forest moon of Endor for 42 seasons. When his Ewok tribe captures a Rebel Alliance strike force, Chirpa is only stopped from sacrificing them by C-3PO, whom the superstitious Ewoks believe is a "golden god."

The Bright Tree tribe lives in a village high up in the treetops.

Hood

Chief's medallion

Hunting knife

Reptilian staff

DATA FILE

AFFILIATION: Republic/ Rebel Alliance

HOMEWORLD: Endor

SPECIES: Ewok

HEIGHT: 1 m (3 ft 3 in)

APPEARANCES: VI

SEE ALSO: Logray; Teebo

New Recruits

After listening to C-3PO's account of the resistance to the Empire, Chirpa commits the Ewoks to the struggle. In the Battle of Endor, the Ewok warriors use all their cunning and fierceness to defeat the superior forces of the Imperial army.

Chirpa leads his people with understanding, though he has become a bit forgetful in his old age. His authority commits the Ewoks to their dangerous fight against the Empire.

CIN DRALLIG
JEDI SWORDMASTER

JEDI MASTER CIN DRALLIG is swordmaster at the Jedi Temple. Jedi Master Yoda personally trained him; the talented Drallig goes on to teach lightsaber combat to many students, including Obi-Wan Kenobi and Anakin Skywalker.

Drallig and many more Jedi, old and young, die in Vader's terrible raid on the Jedi Temple.

Ready stance

Jedi robe

Utility pouch

Plain trousers

DATA FILE

AFFILIATION: Jedi
HOMEWORLD: Lavisar
SPECIES: Human
HEIGHT: 1.77 m (5 ft 8 in)
APPEARANCES: III
SEE ALSO: Yoda; Obi-Wan
Kenobi; Anakin Skywalker

Despite being the Temple's finest swordmaster at the time of Darth Vader's raid on the Jedi Temple, even the esteemed Cin Drallig is unable to defeat a raging Sith Lord in combat.

Vader's Rampage

A security camera in the Jedi Temple records Drallig's death at the hands of Darth Vader. Yoda and Obi-Wan Kenobi find his body when they return to the Temple to reset the emergency beacon to warn all surviving Jedi to flee into exile.

CLIEGG LARS

SHMI SKYWALKER'S HUSBAND

WHEN TATOOINIAN moisture farmer Cliegg Lars goes looking for a farmhand in Mos Espa, he meets instead a slave and falls in love. The slave is Shmi Skywalker, Anakin Skywalker's mother. In order to marry Shmi, Cliegg buys her freedom from Watto, the flying junk dealer who owns her.

Cliegg loses a leg in his attempt to rescue Shmi from Tusken Raiders.

DATA FILE

AFFILIATION: Republic
HOMEWORLD: Tatooine
SPECIES: Human
HEIGHT:
  1.83 m (6 ft)
APPEARANCES: II
SEE ALSO:
  Shmi Skywalker;
  Owen Lars;
  Beru Lars

Control stick

Footrest

Heartbroken

Cliegg loses Shmi when Tusken Raiders kidnap and kill her. After her death, Cliegg remains determined to live the life he has worked so hard to create. Sadly, he dies shortly afterward from his injured leg and a broken heart.

Cliegg's father was a Tatooine farmer, but young Cliegg wanted to experience life on a bustling Core World. Here, he married Aika and had a son, Owen. But when Aika died, he returned to Tatooine to run the family farm.

CLONE PILOT
SPECIALIST CLONE AIRMEN

FROM THE START of the Clone Wars, clones were trained to fly LAAT gunships. As the war progresses, a new breed are trained to fly the hyperspace-capable ARC-170 and V-wing starfighters.

A pilot and copilot/forward gunner fly an ARC-170 fighter at the Battle of Coruscant.

Anti-glare blast visor

Air-supply hose

Rebreather unit

Flight data records pouch

DATA FILE

AFFILIATION:
Republic/Empire
SPECIES: Human
STANDARD EQUIPMENT:
DC-15S blaster; thermal detonators; ammunition
APPEARANCES: II, III, CW
SEE ALSO: Clone trooper

In the Battle
of Coruscant, most clone pilots wear Phase II pilot armor, with helmets fitted with anti-glare blast visors. V-wing pilots, however, wear fully enclosed helmets since these ships carry no on-board life support systems.

Gunship Pilots
At the start of the Clone Wars, in the Battle of Geonosis, clone pilots fly LAAT/i and LAAT/c gunships. They wear Phase I battle armor, distinguished by yellow markings and specialized full-face helmets.

CLONE TROOPER (PHASE I)
FIRST GENERATION CLONE TROOPERS

THE FIRST CLONE troopers are known as Phase I for their style of armor. Born and raised in the cloning factories on Kamino, they are trained for no other purpose than to fight and feel virtually invincible.

Clone troopers are deployed from Republic assault ships, which also carry gunships.

Breath filter

DC-15 blaster

First Strike

When the Separatist droid army makes its first all-out strike on Geonosis, the Senate has no choice but to send in an army of clone soldiers that it has neither amassed nor trained. Under the skillful command of the Jedi, the clones force a droid retreat.

DATA FILE

AFFILIATION: Republic
HOMEWORLD: Kamino
SPECIES: Human
HEIGHT: 1.83 m (6 ft)
APPEARANCES: II, CW
SEE ALSO: Clone trooper (Phase II); Clone pilot; Jango Fett

Thigh plate

Utility belt

Phase I armor is loosely based on Jango Fett's Mandalorian shock trooper armor. It consists of 20 armor plates and is often referred to as the "body bucket" because it is heavy and uncomfortable.

High-traction soles

CLONE TROOPER (PHASE II)

SECOND GENERATION CLONE TROOPERS

BY THE TIME OF the Battle of Coruscant, clone troopers, with enhanced Phase II armor, are battle-dented and mud-smeared. Aging at twice the rate of normally birthed humans, only two-thirds of the original army of clone troopers are alive. Clones are also being grown on other worlds, with cells from new templates.

Clone troops form the galaxy's best military force.

Superior Troopers

Clone troopers are equipped with far more advanced armor and air support than the Separatists, allowing them to easily cut through the battle droid ranks.

Battle-damaged chest plastron

Spare blaster magazine

Knee plate

DATA FILE

AFFILIATION: Republic/ Empire

HOMEWORLD: Kamino

SPECIES: Human

HEIGHT: 1.83 m (6 ft)

APPEARANCES: III, CW

SEE ALSO: Clone trooper (Phase I)

Phase II

armor is stronger, lighter, and more adaptable than Phase I armor, and has many specialist variations.

Standard DC-15 blaster has a folding stock

COLEMAN TREBOR

VURK JEDI MASTER

JEDI MASTER Coleman Trebor is revered as a skillful mediator, bringing difficult disputes to a harmonious end. His skill with a lightsaber is also impressive, and he joins Dooku's taskforce to Geonosis.

Coleman Trebor joined the Jedi High Council after the death of Yarael Poof.

Bony head crest grows through life

Thick reptilian skin

Facing Dooku

On Geonosis, Coleman Trebor seizes his opportunity and steps up to Count Dooku, taking the Separatist leader by surprise. But bounty hunter Jango Fett quickly fires his blaster at the noble Jedi, who falls to his death.

Food and energy capsules

DATA FILE

AFFILIATION: Jedi
HOMEWORLD: Sembla
SPECIES: Vurk
HEIGHT: 2.13 m (6 ft 12 in)
APPEARANCES: II
SEE ALSO: Yarael Poof; Count Dooku

Coleman Trebor is a Vurk from the oceanic world of Sembla. His species is thought to be primitive, but they are in fact highly empathetic and serene. Trebor's Force potential was spotted early on, and he joined the Jedi Order, the only Vurk known to have done so.

Jedi cloak

COLO CLAW FISH

NABOO SEA MONSTERS

THIS SERPENTINE PREDATOR, found in Naboo's lakes, is adapted to swallow prey larger than its own head. Its jaws can distend and its skin can stretch to engulf astonishingly large creatures. A claw fish attacks Qui-Gon Jinn, Obi-Wan Kenobi, and Jar Jar Binks when they travel to Theed by bongo sub.

Colos live in the depths of Naboo's seas surrounding the underwater city of Otoh Gunga.

DATA FILE

HOMEWORLD: Naboo
LENGTH: 40 m (131 ft 3 in)
DIET: Carnivorous
HABITAT: Lakes, oceans
APPEARANCES: I
SEE ALSO: Opee sea killer; sando aqua monster

Brutal Fangs

The colo digests its food slowly, using weak stomach acids. It must be certain to stun prey with its venomous fangs before swallowing, to avoid the creature eating its way out of the colo's stomach to safety.

Nodules attract prey

Pectoral claws

Colos disorientate prey by uttering a weird, hydrosonic shriek using special structures in its throat and head. The colo then seizes the prey with its huge pectoral claws, for which it is named.

Venomous fangs

Baby colo claw fish

COMMANDER BACARA
KI-ADI-MUNDI'S CLONE COMMANDER

CLONE COMMANDER Bacara (also known as CC-1138) received ARC training. The ARC program turns ordinary clones into leaders, by developing their individual thinking. Bacara serves Jedi Master Ki-Adi-Mundi.

Bacara and snow armor-clad Galactic Marines fight on Mygeeto.

Before taking part in ARC training, Bacara was one of the few clones who trained with an ex-Journeyman Protector (lawmen on Jango Fett's homeworld, Concord Dawn) rather than with Fett's hand-picked Mandalorian instructors. For some, this explains Bacara's reputation as a loner.

Blizzard protection side plates

DC-15 blaster rifle

Utility belt

Kneecap armor

Battle of Mygeeto

Commander Bacara fights alongside Ki-Adi-Mundi in many battles. At the end of the Clone Wars, the two warriors travel to the snow-covered world of Mygeeto, where Republic forces have been fighting droids for two years. Bacara leads his fellow marines through Mygeeto's cities.

DATA FILE

AFFILIATION: Republic/Empire
HOMEWORLD: Kamino
SPECIES: Human
HEIGHT: 1.83 m (6 ft)
APPEARANCES: III
SEE ALSO: Ki-Adi-Mundi; clone trooper (Phase II)

COMMANDER BLY

AAYLA SECURA'S CLONE COMMANDER

COMMANDER BLY is a clone of Jango Fett. He was part of the first wave of clone commanders trained by the Advanced Recon Commando (ARC) troopers. Bly's focus is entirely on the success of each mission.

After Order 66 turned him against the Republic, Bly served the Empire.

Helmet contains oxygen supply

Color denotes legion affiliation

DATA FILE

AFFILIATION: Republic/ Empire
HOMEWORLD: Kamino
SPECIES: Human
HEIGHT: 1.83 m (6 ft)
APPEARANCES: III, CW
SEE ALSO: Aayla Secura; clone trooper (Phase II); Jango Fett

Quick-release holster for DC-17 repeater hand blaster

Cold Commander

Clone Commander Bly and Jedi General Aayla Secura are hunting down Separatist leader Shu Mai on the exotic world of Felucia when Bly receives Palpatine's Order 66. Without a second's hesitation, the clone soldier guns down the Jedi Knight he had served with on so many perilous missions.

Clone Commander

CC-5052, or Bly, has worked closely with Jedi General Aayla Secura, and respects her dedication to completing the mission.

High-traction boots

Plastoid armor pitted from shrapnel strikes

COMMANDER CODY

OBI-WAN KENOBI'S CLONE COMMANDER

CLONE UNIT 2224, known as Commander Cody, is often assigned to Jedi General Obi-Wan Kenobi. He is one of the original clones from Kamino. His extra training developed leadership ability.

Cody's last loyal action: returning Kenobi's lost lightsaber to the Jedi.

Breath filter

DC-15A standard blaster

DATA FILE

AFFILIATION: Republic/ Empire
SPECIES: Human
HOMEWORLD: Kamino
HEIGHT: 1.83 m (6 ft)
APPEARANCES: III, CW
SEE ALSO: Clone trooper; Obi-Wan Kenobi

Sidious in Charge

Cody fights loyally and bravely alongside General Kenobi on many missions in the Clone Wars, including on Lola Sayu and Utapau. They have established an easy-going camaraderie. Nevertheless, when Cody receives Palpatine's Order 66 to kill the Jedi, he does so without giving his betrayal a second thought.

Plastoid armor dented with shrapnel strikes

Color denotes legion affiliation

High-traction boots

Clone commanders like Cody use names in addition to numerical designations. The Jedi and progressive-thinking Republic officials initiated this practice in order to foster a growing fellowship. This is why CC-2224 came to be called Cody.

COMMANDER GREE
SENIOR CLONE COMMANDER OF KASHYYYK

CLONE COMANDER GREE commands the 41st Elite Corps in the Clone Wars. Led by Jedi General Luminara Unduli, the 41st specializes in long-term missions on alien worlds. Gree uses his knowledge of the customs of alien species to help build alliances with local populations.

Ultimately loyal only to Palpatine, Gree attempts to kill Yoda. But Yoda strikes down the clone.

Polarized T-visor

DATA FILE

AFFILIATION: Republic
HOMEWORLD: Kamino
SPECIES: Human
HEIGHT: 1.83 m (6 ft)
APPEARANCES: III, CW
SEE ALSO: Yoda; Luminara Unduli

Camouflage markings

Wookiee Defenders

Gree serves under Jedi Master Yoda at the Battle of Kashyyyk. Gree's camouflage armor provides cover in the green jungles of the Wookiee planet. His battle-hardened clone troopers are also equipped for jungle warfare.

Clone unit 1004 chose the name Gree to express his interest in the wide and varied alien cultures found throughout the galaxy. The Gree is a little-known alien species.

Weapons and ammunition belt

Reinforced tactical boots

Armor plates are often replaced

COMMANDER NEYO
STASS ALLIE'S CLONE COMMANDER

CLONE COMMANDER NEYO is assigned to the 91st Reconnaissance Corps, which often utilizes BARC speeders. Neyo fights many battles in the Outer Rim sieges during the Clone Wars.

Neyo serves with Jedi Stass Allie in the siege of the Separatist planet Saleucami.

Enhanced breath filter

Built-in comlink

Equipment pouch

Regiment markings

Neyo, or unit 8826, is one of the first 100 graduates from the experimental clone commander training program on Kamino. Bred solely for fighting, Neyo developed a disturbingly cold personality.

ARC command sash

DATA FILE

AFFILIATION: Republic/ Empire
SPECIES: Human
HOMEWORLD: Kamino
HEIGHT: 1.83 m (6 ft)
APPEARANCES: III
SEE ALSO: Stass Allie; clone trooper (Phase II)

Clone Betrayal

After the Republic captures Saleucami, Neyo stays on to destroy the last pockets of resistance. During a speeder patrol with Stass Allie, Neyo receives Order 66 and turns his laser cannons on the Jedi General.

COUNT DOOKU
SEPARATIST LEADER AND SITH LORD

COUNT DOOKU was once a Jedi Master. But his independent spirit led him away from the Order and he became a Sith apprentice, named Darth Tyranus. As Dooku, he leads the Separatist movement, which seeks independence from the Republic.

Caught between Anakin's blades, Dooku is unprepared for Sidious' treachery.

Count Dooku is a member of the nobility on his homeworld of Serenno and one of the richest men in the galaxy. He uses his wealth and power to convince many star systems to join his Separatist movement.

Cape is emblem of Count of Serenno

Curved lightsaber

Belt contains comlink and secret weapons

Underlayer made of costly fabric

Sith Skills

Count Dooku is a formidable opponent. He is a master of ancient Form II lightsaber combat, characterized by graceful moves. He can also project deadly streams of Sith Force lightning from his fingertips.

Boots of rare rancor leather

DATA FILE

AFFILIATION: Sith
HOMEWORLD: Serenno
SPECIES: Human
HEIGHT: 1.93 m (6 ft 4 in)
APPEARANCES: II, III, CW
SEE ALSO: Palpatine; Anakin Skywalker

CRAB DROID

SIX-LEGGED BATTLE DROIDS

KNOWN TO CLONE TROOPERS as "Muckrackers," Separatist crab droids are deployed during the Clone Wars on marshy worlds such as Utapau. These heavily armored weapons are made in a range of sizes, from small spy drones to huge trailblazers. Crab droids can also push their way through muck to create paths for infantry.

Developed during the Clone Wars, the Techno Union produces large numbers of crab droids.

DATA FILE

AFFILIATION: Separatist
HEIGHT: 1.49 m (4 ft 11 in)
APPEARANCES: III, CW
SEE ALSO: Battle droid;
dwarf spider droid

Weak Spot

Crab droids prove to be a threat against the clone troopers during the Battle of Utapau. However, some brave troopers escape the droid's targeting sensors and find its weak spots behind the forward armor.

Armorplast shielding

Sensor bulb

Duranium stabilizer can push through bedrock

Twin blasters

Crab droids' powerful legs allow them to scuttle at high speeds on uneven terrain and even up craggy surfaces. Their front pincers also serve as vacuums, slurping up and spewing out lake-bed mud.

DARTH MAUL
SITH APPRENTICE

DARTH MAUL IS Darth Sidious's apprentice and one of the most dangerous and highly trained Sith in the history of the Order. His entire body is tattooed with symbols that show his heritage of the warrior tribe known as the Nightbrothers of Dathomir.

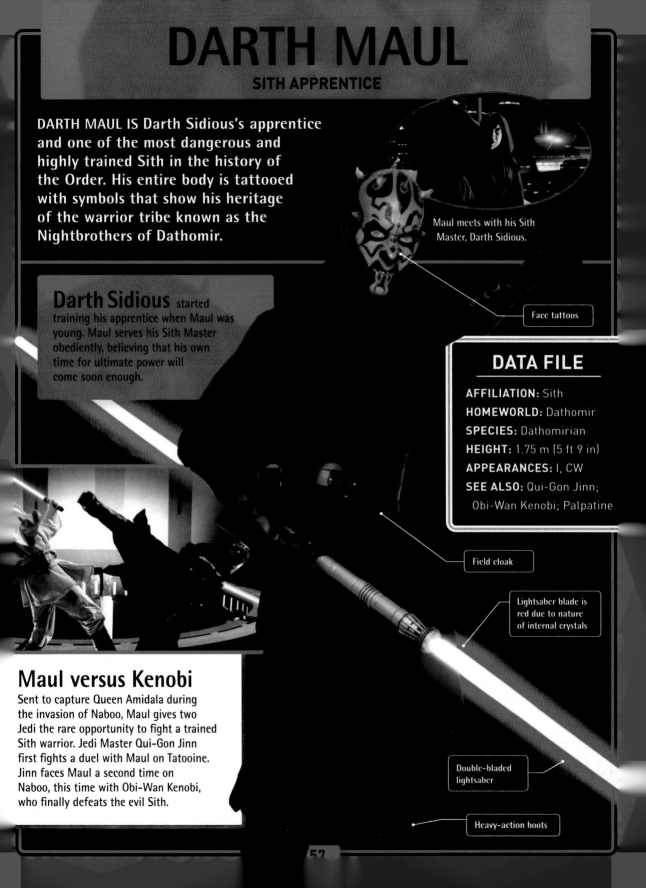

Maul meets with his Sith Master, Darth Sidious.

Face tattoos

Darth Sidious started training his apprentice when Maul was young. Maul serves his Sith Master obediently, believing that his own time for ultimate power will come soon enough.

DATA FILE

AFFILIATION: Sith
HOMEWORLD: Dathomir
SPECIES: Dathomirian
HEIGHT: 1.75 m (5 ft 9 in)
APPEARANCES: I, CW
SEE ALSO: Qui-Gon Jinn;
   Obi-Wan Kenobi; Palpatine

Field cloak

Lightsaber blade is red due to nature of internal crystals

Maul versus Kenobi

Sent to capture Queen Amidala during the invasion of Naboo, Maul gives two Jedi the rare opportunity to fight a trained Sith warrior. Jedi Master Qui-Gon Jinn first fights a duel with Maul on Tatooine. Jinn faces Maul a second time on Naboo, this time with Obi-Wan Kenobi, who finally defeats the evil Sith.

Double-bladed lightsaber

Heavy-action boots

DARTH VADER

DARK LORD OF THE SITH

THE GRIM, FORBIDDING figure of Darth Vader is Emperor Palpatine's Sith apprentice and a much-feared military commander. Vader's knowledge of the dark side of the Force makes him unnerving and dangerous.

Darth Vader fights the battle that will result in his encasement in a life-supporting suit.

Voice projector/ respiratory intake

Control function panel

System function display

DATA FILE

AFFILIATION: Sith
HOMEWORLD: Tatooine
SPECIES: Human
HEIGHT: (armored) 2.02 m (6 ft 7 in)
APPEARANCES: III, IV, V, VI
SEE ALSO: Palpatine; Luke Skywalker

Father and Son

When Vader learns that Luke Skywalker is his son, he harbors a desire to turn Luke to the dark side and rule the galaxy with him. Yet Luke refuses to lose sight of Vader's humanity under the armor.

Sith blade

Outer cloak

After Vader's

near-fatal duel with Obi-Wan Kenobi on Mustafar, Palpatine has his apprentice encased in black armor. Vader is unable to survive without the constant life support provided by his black suit.

DEATH STAR GUNNER

IMPERIAL WEAPONS OPERATORS

DEATH STAR GUNNERS control the terrible weapons of the Empire's capital ships, military bases, and Death Star battlestations. Their elite skills with weapons are used to handle powerful turbolasers and ion cannons.

Gunners on platforms monitor the titanic energy levels of the Death Star's superlaser.

Helmet protects eyes from bright flashes from enemy fire

DATA FILE

AFFILIATION: Empire
SPECIES: Human
AVERAGE HEIGHT: 1.8 m (5 ft 11 in)
APPEARANCES: IV, VI
SEE ALSO: AT-AT pilot; AT-ST pilot; stormtrooper

Turbolaser Gunners

The Empire's capital ships and its Death Star are bristling with turbolasers. A team of gunners man these heavy guns, which rotate on turrets. The gunners monitor crucial recharge timings and heat levels, while locking onto targets. A single blast can obliterate an enemy starfighter.

Energy-shielded fabric

The Imperial Navy

equips Death Star gunners with specialized helmets with slit-like visors, designed to protect their eyes from the bright flashes of light from turbolaser and superlaser fire. Many gunners find that the helmets restrict all-round vision.

Positive gravity pressure boots

DEPA BILLABA

JEDI HIGH COUNCIL MEMBER

JEDI MASTER Depa Billaba serves on the Jedi High Council and goes on missions to Nar Shaddaa and Haruun Kal. In the stresses of battle, Depa succumbs to the dark side of the Force.

Billaba offers an ordered perspective to the wide-ranging minds of her fellow Jedi.

Chalactan marks of illumination

Jedi robes cover practical fighting tunic

Billaba is of the few masters of the challenging Form VII: Vaapad lightsaber technique that Mace Windu created

Jedi Fellowship

Jedi Master Mace Windu rescued Billaba from the space pirates who killed her parents. Eventually, Windu took Billaba as his Padawan. Over the years, they have developed a close bond.

Lightsaber worn on utility belt under robes

DATA FILE

AFFILIATION: Jedi
HOMEWORLD: Chalacta
SPECIES: Chalactan
HEIGHT: 1.68 m (5 ft 6 in)
APPEARANCES: I, II
SEE ALSO: Mace Windu; Yoda; Qui-Gon Jinn

Depa Billaba is

wise and spiritual. She practices the traditional culture of her planet, Chalacta, in honor of her parents. However, Depa fought in a brutal guerrilla war on Mace Windu's homeworld, Haruun Kal, and fell to the dark side.

DEWBACK
TATOOINIAN REPTILES

LARGE DEWBACK LIZARDS live on the desert planet Tatooine. Locals use them for carrying heavy loads and as transport. During the time of the Empire, Imperial sandtroopers ride dewbacks on Tatooine in preference to their mechanical vehicles, which are more easily harmed by sand and heat.

C-3PO and R2-D2 look on nervously while a sandtrooper dismounts to interrogate a local.

Search Patrol

A squad of sandtroopers search the desert for signs of the droids who escaped from Princess Leia's ship with stolen Death Star plans. Imperial sandtroopers often ride dewbacks when carrying out security and military patrols.

DATA FILE

HOMEWORLD: Tatooine
HEIGHT: 1.8 m (5 ft 11 in)
DIET: Omnivorous
HABITAT: Desert
APPEARANCES: I, VI
SEE ALSO: Sandtrooper

Saddle harnessed to dewback

Dewbacks are solitary by nature and can be found roaming the desert in small packs of two to five. During the day, they forage for food and moisture. When the temperature drops at night, they become sluggish and huddle together to keep warm.

Powerful, load-bearing haunches

Body adapted for living in desert

Claws

DEXTER JETTSTER

BESALISK COOK AND INFORMANT

THE FOUR-ARMED Besalisk named Dexter
Jettster runs a diner on Coruscant. Dexter is an
individual with diverse connections. This is why
Obi-Wan Kenobi seeks him out when he needs
information on a mysterious
toxic saberdart that has killed
assassin Zam Wesell.

Dexter is chief cook and bottle washer in his
diner in an unfashionable part of Coruscant.

Male Besalisk crest

The gruff but good-
hearted Dexter Jettster spent
many years manning oil rigs across
the galaxy, tending bar,
brawling, and running
weapons on the side.
On Coruscant, he has
made a fresh start
with his diner.

Informant

Beneath his sloppy exterior, Dexter has a
keen sense of observation and a retentive
memory. He can serve up vital information,
even to the likes of a Jedi Knight such
as Obi-Wan Kenobi.

**Powerful
arm**

**Dexterous
fingers**

DATA FILE

AFFILIATION:
Republic
HOMEWORLD:
Ojom
SPECIES: Besalisk
HEIGHT: 1.9 m
(6 ft 6 in)
APPEARANCES: II
SEE ALSO: Obi-Wan Kenobi

DOCTOR EVAZAN

MURDEROUS CRIMINAL

CARRYING MULTIPLE DEATH sentences, the murderous Doctor Evazan is notorious for rearranging body parts on living creatures. Evazan and his partner, Ponda Baba, also enjoy brawling and gunning down defenseless beings.

Evazan and Ponda Baba pull blasters: Bartender Wuher ducks, but Kenobi stands his ground.

Facial scarring

DATA FILE

AFFILIATION: Non-affiliated
HOMEWORLD: Alsakan
SPECIES: Human
HEIGHT: 1.7 m (5 ft 7 in)
APPEARANCES: IV
SEE ALSO: Ponda Baba

Weapons belt

Holster

Criminal Thug

Evazan is a smuggler and murderer with many enemies across the galaxy. A bounty hunter once tried to kill Evazan, scarring his face. An Aqualish trouble-maker named Ponda Baba saved him and became his partner in crime.

Evazan was once a promising surgeon. However, during his training he was corrupted by madness. He now practices "creative surgery" (without the assistance of droids) on hundreds of victims, leaving them hideously scarred.

DROIDEKA
DESTROYER DROIDS

DROIDEKAS ARE HEAVY DUTY destroying machines that back up battle droids in the face of determined opposition. They uncoil in a matter of seconds from wheel form into standing position, ready to attack. They also carry their own deflector shield generators to protect from enemy fire.

For optimum travel speed, droidekas retract into the shape of a wheel.

Sensor head

Fearsome Droids

Covered with heavy alloy or armor plate, droidekas cut down soldiers by the dozen with ease. Their deflector shield generators can completely repel pistol fire and weaken high-energy bolts.

Twin blaster

Mini-reactor bulb

Moving leg

DATA FILE

AFFILIATION: Separatist
TYPE: Destroyer droid
MANUFACTURER: Colicoids
HEIGHT: 1.83 m (6 ft)
APPEARANCES: I, II, III, CW
SEE ALSO: Battle droid; super battle droid

A species of insectoid Colicoids on the planet Colla IV created the design of the droideka in their own image. Colicoids are known for their completely unfeeling and murderous ways. The Trade Federation initially paid the Colicoids in exotic meats for shipments of the droids.

DROOPY McCOOL

HORN PLAYER IN THE MAX REBO BAND

DROOPY MCCOOL IS THE stage name of Snit, the lead horn player in the Max Rebo Band, Jabba's house band. A far-out quasi-mystic Kitonak, Droopy's real name is a series of flute-like whistles, unpronounceable by any other species.

After Jabba's death, McCool disappears into the desert.

Tiny eyes

Chidinkalu flute

Body releases a vanilla-like smell

Jamming

Laidback Droopy is largely oblivious to what is going on around him. He hardly recognizes the stage name that Max Rebo gave him—Droopy just plays the tunes.

McCool is

lonely for the company of his own kind and claims to have heard the faint tones of other Kitonaks somewhere out in the Tatooine dunes.

DATA FILE

AFFILIATION: Jabba's entourage
HOMEWORLD: Kirdo III
SPECIES: Kitonak
HEIGHT: 1.6 m (5 ft 2 in)
APPEARANCES: VI
SEE ALSO: Max Rebo; Jabba the Hutt

Tough, leathery skin

DWARF SPIDER DROID

FOUR-LEGGED BATTLE DROIDS

COMMERCE GUILD DWARF SPIDER DROIDS are more rugged than battle droids. Their four striding legs are designed for roadless terrain on rocky mining worlds. They are armed with head-mounted blaster cannons that are effective against infantry troops, and they can also easily destroy small vehicles.

Devastating firepower is the dwarf spider droid's strength; it is vulnerable from behind.

DATA FILE

AFFILIATION: Separatist
TYPE: Battle droid
MANUFACTURER: Baktoid Armor Workshop
HEIGHT: 1.98 m (6 ft 6 in)
APPEARANCES: II, CW
SEE ALSO: Battle droid; homing spider droid

Dwarf spider droids speak a form of binary droid language, and sometimes express frustration. If threatened on the battlefield, these dangerous droids can trigger a self-destruct mechanism.

Primary laser cannon

Clawed feet can climb up cliffs

Photoreceptors see in infrared

Armored body core

Hunters

Dwarf spider droids are first used for warfare at the Battle of Geonosis. Until this time, the Commerce Guild used the droids to scuttle down narrow mine shafts to enforce tribute payments.

66

EETH KOTH

JEDI HIGH COUNCIL MEMBER

JEDI MASTER AND JEDI High Council member Eeth Koth is an Iridonian Zabrak. This horned species is known for its determination and mental discipline, which enables individuals to tolerate great physical suffering.

Koth and his fellow Jedi must judge whether Anakin should start training.

Vestigial horns

Jedi tunic

Traditional leather utility belt

Late Starter

Koth started his Jedi training at the unusually late age of four years, making him more receptive than his fellow council members to Qui-Gon Jinn's appeal to train Anakin Skywalker.

DATA FILE

AFFILIATION: Jedi
HOMEWORLD:
  Nar Shaddaa
SPECIES: Iridonian Zabrak
HEIGHT: 1.71 m (5 ft 7 in)
APPEARANCES: I, II, CW
SEE ALSO: Mace Windu;
  Plo Koon

Loose sleeves allow freedom of movement

Long, loose robes

Eeth Koth partners with other Jedi on many missions, including Plo Koon. He also shares a Concordance of Fealty with Mace Windu, in which they swap lightsabers as an act of trust.

ELAN SLEAZEBAGGANO

CORUSCANT SLYTHMONGER

THE SLIMY LOW-LIFE known as Elan Sleazebaggano is a notorious "slythmonger." He cruises the Coruscant nightclubs trying to sell cheap narcotics manufactured by disbarred pharmacists.

Elan sells "death sticks," with powerful cilona extract that literally shorten users' lifespans.

Fashionable choker

Casual shirt

Long overcoat conceals illegal chemicals for sale

DATA FILE

AFFILIATION: Republic
HOMEWORLD: Coruscant
SPECIES: Balosar
HEIGHT: 1.78 m (5 ft 10 in)
APPEARANCES: II
SEE ALSO: Obi-Wan Kenobi

Shoes contain secret storage compartments for contraband

Power of the Force

When Elan tries to sell death sticks to Obi-Wan Kenobi in a Coruscant nightclub, the Jedi uses the Force to suggest that he rethink his life. Elan does this for a while, but soon drifts back into his old life of crime.

Elan is a Balosar, a humanoid species with antennapalps (flexible ear stalks) that grow from their heads. These highly sensitive organs operate at a subsonic level, and appear to give Balosars special powers of intuition.

EV-9D9

SADISTIC DROID SUPERVISOR

EV-9D9 IS JABBA THE HUTT'S droid overseer in the murky depths of his palace on Tatooine. EV-9D9's programming is corrupted, and she works Jabba's droids until they fall apart, employing bizarre forms of droid torture to increase motivation.

EV-9D9 added a third eye to herself to "see" droid pain.

Degraded logic center

DATA FILE

AFFILIATION: Jabba's entourage
TYPE: Supervisor droid
MANUFACTURER: MerenData
HEIGHT: 1.9 m (6 ft 3 in)
APPEARANCES: VI
SEE ALSO: 8D8; C-3PO; R2-D2

Supervisor

As Jabba's droid overseer, EV-9D9 assigns C-3PO as Hutt's translator and R2-D2 as drinks waiter on Jabba's sail barge.

Custom-fitted third eye

Manipulator arm

EV-9D9 is not the only EV unit with the programming defect that causes her cruel behavior—many have the same flaw. But she is one of the few to escape the mass recall. EV-9D9 now relishes her role as taskmaster of all droids at the palace.

EVEN PIELL

LANNIK JEDI MASTER

THIS OUTSPOKEN JEDI MASTER is not to be underestimated. Even Piell bears a scar across his eye as a grisly trophy of a victory against terrorists who made the mistake of thinking too little of the undersized Jedi.

Seated next to Yoda, Even Piell has one of the long-term seats on the Jedi High Council.

Jedi topknot

Large ears sensitive in thin atmosphere

Momentous Events

Even Piell sits on the Jedi High Council during the galaxy's first steps toward war. He is present when Qui-Gon Jinn presents the young Anakin Skywalker to the esteemed Jedi leaders for the first time.

DATA FILE

AFFILIATION: Jedi
HOMEWORLD: Lannik
SPECIES: Lannik
HEIGHT: 1.22 m (4 ft)
APPEARANCES: I, II, CW
SEE ALSO: Yoda; Anakin Skywalker; Qui-Gon Jinn

Piell is from Lannik, a planet with a long history of war. A gruff and battle-hardened warrior during the Clone Wars, Piell is taken prisoner and held captive at the infamous Citadel Station. Though mortally wounded during his escape, he is able to transfer vital information crucial to the war effort to Ahsoka Tano.

FIGRIN D'AN

BITH BAND LEADER

DEMON KLOO HORN PLAYER Figrin D'an is the frontman for the Modal Nodes, a group of seven Bith musicians. They play in various venues on Tatooine, including Chalmun's Cantina in Mos Eisley and Jabba the Hutt's desert palace.

A Wookiee named Chalmun owns the cantina in which the Modal Nodes play.

Large eyes

Enlarged cranium

Kloo horn

Tone mode selectors

Band Members

The Modal Nodes are Figrin D'an on kloo horn, Doikk Na'ts on Dorenian Beshniquel (or Fizzz), Ickabel G'ont on the Double Jocimer, Tedn Dahai on fanfar, Tech Mo'r on the Ommni Box, Nalan Cheel on the bandfill, and Sun'il Ei'de on the drums. Lirin Car'n often sits in to play second kloo horn.

DATA FILE

AFFILIATION: Non-affiliated
HOMEWORLD: Clak'dor VII
SPECIES: Bith
HEIGHT: 1.5 m (4 ft 11 in)
APPEARANCES: IV
SEE ALSO: Jabba the Hutt

Band pants

Travel boots

Figrin is a demanding band leader, who expects the best from his musicians. His overbearing nature has earned him the nickname "Fiery" Figrin D'an. As well as playing the kloo horn, Figrin is a compulsive card shark who frequently gambles the band's earnings.

FX-SERIES MED DROID

MEDICAL ASSISTANT DROIDS

MEDICAL DROIDS OF ALL TYPES are equipped with huge memory banks to allow them to choose the best course of treatment in any situation. FX-series droids act as medical assistants. They monitor patients and operate equipment.

An FX-9 surgical assistant performs many blood transfusions during Vader's reconstruction.

Medical data banks

High-speed data output transmitter

Bioelectrical sensor arm

Pressure test arm

Life Saver

In the medical center within the Rebel base on Hoth, an FX-7 med droid monitors Luke Skywalker's injuries while he is immersed in a bacta tank. The synthetic chemical bacta heals flesh wounds. FX-7 checks that the bacta mix is properly filtered and vitalized.

Equipment operator arm

DATA FILE

AFFILIATION: Droid
TYPE: FX-series droid
MANUFACTURER:
 Medtech Industries
HEIGHT: Varies
APPEARANCES: III, V
SEE ALSO: 2-1B;
 Luke Skywalker

FX-series droids have arms which can rapidly check the condition of a patient by performing various tests suited to different species. These droids work alongside surgeon droids, providing the surgeon with the information they need to perform appropriate treatments.

GAMORREAN GUARD
SENTRIES AT JABBA'S PALACE

TOUGH, BRUTISH Gamorrean guards stand throughout Jabba's Tatooine palace as sentries. These stocky, slow-witted, green-skinned creatures are stubborn and loyal, though prone to outbursts of barbaric violence.

Gamorreans are willing spectators to the casual violence at Jabba's palace.

Weak eyes

Fangs

DATA FILE

AFFILIATION: Jabba's entourage
HOMEWORLD: Gamorr
HEIGHT: 1.7 m (5 ft 7 in)
APPEARANCES: VI, CW
SEE ALSO: Jabba the Hutt

Gauntlet

Fit for Duty
The low intelligence of the Gamorreans makes them almost impossible to bribe, which is an asset to their masters. Their preferred weapons are axes and vibro-lances rather than blasters.

Heavy-duty ax head

Gamorreans come from the warlike Outer Rim planet Gamorr. Male Gamorreans, named boars, either fight terrible wars or prepare for war, while the female sows farm and hunt.

Leather sandals

GARINDAN

MOS EISLEY SPY

GARINDAN IS A GREEDY and immoral Kubaz from the planet Kubindi. He is a paid informant who works for the highest bidder. In Mos Eisley, the Imperial authorities hire Garindan to locate two missing droids. The low-life spy quickly picks up the trail of Luke Skywalker, Obi-Wan Kenobi, R2-D2, and C-3PO.

Garindan has a long trunk, which he uses to dine on his favorite delicacy: insects.

DATA FILE

AFFILIATION: Non-affiliated
HOMEWORLD: Kubindi
SPECIES: Kubaz
HEIGHT: 1.85 m (6 ft 1 in)
APPEARANCES: IV
SEE ALSO: Sandtrooper; Luke Skywalker

On the Scent

Garindan discovers Luke Skywalker and his friends' plan to meet Han Solo at docking bay 94. Following the group, the sneaky spy then uses his Imperial comlink to call the authorities. When a squad of sandtroopers arrives, Garindan's job is done.

The mysterious

Garindan keeps his face hidden behind a dark hood and goggles. Few individuals know anything much about his private life, which is also hidden in secrecy.

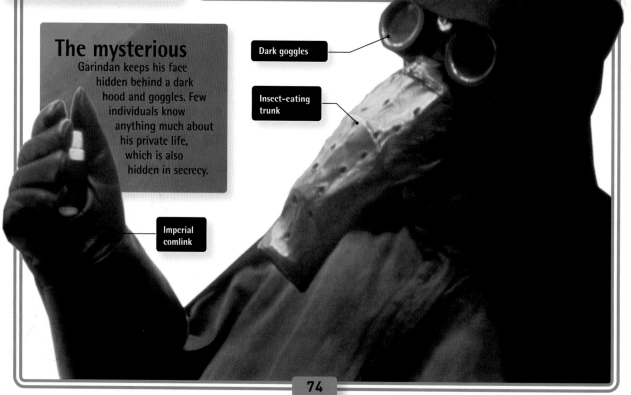

Dark goggles

Insect-eating trunk

Imperial comlink

GENERAL CRACKEN
REBEL INTELLIGENCE AGENT

AIREN CRACKEN is a skilled spy and scout for the Rebel Alliance. He was a general before the Battle of Yavin, and is promoted to Colonel afterward. Cracken also flies support missions for General Madine's Rebel commandos.

At Endor, Lando Calrissian and Nien Nunb pilot the *Falcon*, with Cracken as gunner.

Hands-free comlink

Communications badge

Falcon Gunner

Under the command of General Lando Calrissian at the attack on the second Death Star at the Battle of Endor, General Cracken serves as a gunner on board the *Millennium Falcon*. He mans the upper quad laser cannon.

Lightweight flak vest

Double-magazine canister

Fire-resistant tactical gloves

Cracken learned to use machinery on his parents' farm on Contruum. When the Empire occupied his homeworld, Cracken organized a guerrilla resistance before eventually joining the Rebel Alliance. Cracken oversees a galaxy-wide network of anti-Imperial spies, scouts, and infiltrators.

DATA FILE

AFFILIATION: Rebel Alliance
HOMEWORLD: Contruum
SPECIES: Human
HEIGHT: 1.67 m (5 ft 6 in)
APPEARANCES: VI
SEE ALSO: Lando Calrissian; Admiral Ackbar; Nien Nunb

GENERAL GRIEVOUS
COMMANDER OF THE DROID ARMY

GENERAL GRIEVOUS IS THE Supreme Commander of the Droid Army during the Clone Wars. Grievous reacts furiously to any suggestion that he is a droid. In fact, he is a cyborg: a twisted mix of organic body parts and mechanical armor, with a hunched back and a bad cough.

Grievous's end comes when Obi-Wan Kenobi fires blaster bolts at his vulnerable gutsack.

Reptilian eyes

DATA FILE

AFFILIATION: Separatist
HOMEWORLD: Kalee
SPECIES: Kaleesh
HEIGHT: 2.16 m (7 ft 1 in)
APPEARANCES: III, CW
SEE ALSO: Count Dooku;
   Palpatine; Obi-Wan Kenobi

Grievous is a Kaleesh warlord who was rebuilt after a shuttle crash. The cyborg general is neither Force-sensitive nor a Sith, but Darth Tyranus (Count Dooku) trained him in lightsaber combat.

Electro-driven arms can split in half

Cape contains pockets for lightsabers

Leg drivers house crystal circuitry

Prepared for Battle
After their first battle during the daring rescue of Palpatine, Obi-Wan Kenobi faces Grievous a second time in the Separatist base on Utapau. This time Grievous splits apart his arms in order to wield four lightsabers.

GENERAL MADINE
REBEL COMMANDER AND TACTICIAN

AS COMMANDER of the Rebel Alliance Special Forces, General Madine devises the plan to destroy the Imperial shield generator on Endor's Moon. He also trains the strike force that infiltrates the Moon.

General Madine helps Admiral Ackbar direct the Battle of Endor from the Rebel flagship.

Command insignia

Rebel uniform jerkin

Military gauntlets

Briefing documents

Rebel Advisor

Madine is a respected advisor to the Rebel leader Mon Mothma. Before the Battle of Endor, Madine and Mothma brief their troops on board the Rebel Headquarters frigate, *Home One*. After the fall of the Empire, Madine will serve the New Republic as Chief of Intelligence.

Crix Madine led an Imperial commando unit until his defection to the Alliance. He is an expert in small ground strikes. Madine's unit of Alliance commandos was responsible for the capture of the Imperial shuttle *Tydirium*, in which Solo and his team infiltrate Endor's Moon.

DATA FILE

AFFILIATION: Rebel Alliance
HOMEWORLD: Corellia
SPECIES: Human
HEIGHT: 1.7 m (5 ft 7 in)
APPEARANCES: VI
SEE ALSO: Mon Mothma;
  Admiral Ackbar; Han Solo

GENERAL RIEEKAN
REBEL COMMANDER OF ECHO BASE

GENERAL CARLIST RIEEKAN IS in charge of Echo Base on Hoth. He keeps the seven hidden levels of the base in a state of constant alert, ever wary of discovery by Imperial forces. Rieekan knows that any Rebel activity could be easy to detect in the frozen Hoth system.

Rieekan waits until all other Rebel transports have left Hoth before escaping himself.

DATA FILE

AFFILIATION: Rebel Alliance
HOMEWORLD: Alderaan
SPECIES: Human
HEIGHT: 1.8 m (5 ft 11 in)
APPEARANCES: V
SEE ALSO: Princess Leia

Rebel command insignia

Insulated Rebel uniform jacket

Command gauntlet

Utility belt

Stern Leader

Carlist Rieekan is a decisive commander. When the Imperial army discovers Echo Base, Rieekan plans to delay Vader's forces long enough to give the Rebels time to evacuate the base.

Rieekan was born on Alderaan, Leia Organa's adopted planet. He fought for the Republic in the Clone Wars and became a founding member of the Rebel Alliance. Carlist is off-world when the Death Star superweapon destroys Alderaan, but this terrible event will haunt the Rebel commander ever after.

GENERAL VEERS

GENERAL MAXIMILLIAN Veers is the mastermind behind the devastating Imperial assault on Echo Base. He commands the action in person from within the cockpit of the lead AT-AT walker.

Veers takes aim from inside the cockpit of his AT-AT, codenamed Blizzard One.

Blast helmet

Pilot armor

Utility belt contains mission data

Imperial officer's uniform

Cruel Ambition

Desperate to prove himself to Darth Vader, Veers heads the AT-AT regiment that successfully destroys the Rebel shield power generator, allowing Vader to land on Hoth. Imperial snowtroopers, armed with heavy weapons, then infiltrate Echo Base with frightening speed.

General Veers is

cunning and capable. He has rapidly worked his way up the Imperial ranks. A family man, Veers is viewed as a model Imperial officer. But his sense of infallibility is damaged when his wife dies and his son, Zevulon, joins the Rebellion.

DATA FILE

AFFILIATION: Empire
HOMEWORLD: Denon
SPECIES: Human
HEIGHT: 1.93 m (6 ft 4 in)
APPEARANCES: V
SEE ALSO: Admiral Piett; Admiral Ozzel

GEONOSIAN SOLDIER
SPECIALIZED GEONOSIAN DRONES

GEONOSIAN SOLDIER DRONES are tough and single-minded. They are trained to fight with a fearless attitude, and are highly effective against brute opponents. However, they are poor attackers when faced with intelligent enemies.

Geonosians of all castes watch executions and gladiator battles in huge arenas.

DATA FILE

AFFILIATION: Separatist
HOMEWORLD: Geonosis
SPECIES: Geonosian
HEIGHT: 1.7 m (5 ft 7 in)
APPEARANCES: II, CW
SEE ALSO: Poggle the Lesser; Count Dooku

Prongs protect vulnerable blood vessels

Powerful sonic blaster

Red iketa stone traditionally associated with war

Soldier drones can fly or hover

Well-developed soldier's thigh

Segregation

The caste-segregated planet Geonosis has become the chief supplier of battle droids to the Separatists, led by the aristocratic Count Dooku. Huge foundaries on Geonosis churn out countless droids.

Soldier drones are grown to adulthood rapidly, and can be ready for combat at an age of only six years. They carry sonic blasters, which produce a devastating sonic ball.

GH-7 MEDICAL DROID

MEDICAL ANALYSIS DROIDS

GH-7 MEDDROIDS are all-purpose surgical assistants found in many Outer Rim medical centers. They hover using a compact repulsorlift and employ servoarms to collect specimens or give injections. The droids are softly spoken in order to reassure patients.

A midwife droid assists in the delivery of Padmé Amidala's twins on Polis Massa.

DATA FILE

AFFILIATION: Droid
TYPE: Medical droid
MANUFACTURER:
Chiewab
Amalgamated
Pharmaceuticals
HEIGHT: 0.7 m (2 ft 4 in)
APPEARANCES: III
SEE ALSO: FX-series
med droid; 2-1B

Delivery

On Polis Massa, a GH-7 meddroid reports to Jedi Yoda and Obi-Wan Kenobi. Tragically, the droids are unable to save Padmé's life, despite not finding anything physically wrong with her.

Paired bioscanner

Analysis chamber

Specimen jars

On the remote Outer Rim

world of Polis Massa, meddroids work alongside alien medics, who are actually exobiologists attached to an archeological team working on the planet. Meddroids' bioscanners are linked to computers, which interpret the data and transmit instructions to the droid.

GRAND MOFF TARKIN

ARCHITECT OF THE DEATH STAR

AT THE END of the Clone Wars, Wilhuff Tarkin already has an exalted position as one of Palpatine's regional governors. As Grand Moff Tarkin, he plans the horrific Death Star as part of his doctrine of Rule by Fear.

Tarkin dies on the Death Star when Rebel X-wings cause it to self-destruct.

Code cylinder

Twisted, scheming gesture

Imperial officer's disc

Durasteel-toed boots

Rule by Fear

In order to force Princess Leia to betray the Rebel Alliance, Tarkin orders the destruction of Alderaan by the Death Star. Rather than attempting to police all the scattered individual systems in the Imperial Outlands, Tarkin believes that fear of the Death Star will subjugate systems across the galaxy.

DATA FILE

AFFILIATION: Empire
HOMEWORLD: Eriadu
SPECIES: Human
HEIGHT: 1.8 m (5 ft 11 in)
APPEARANCES: III, IV, CW
SEE ALSO: Palpatine

Tarkin has a history of quelling rebellion by the most cold-blooded means. He also created the role of Grand Moff— officials who have responsibility for stamping out trouble in "priority sectors" across the Empire.

GREEATA
PERFORMER IN THE MAX REBO BAND

GREEATA JENDOWANIAN is a backing singer, dancer, and musician in the Max Rebo Band in Jabba's desert palace. Greeata forms a colorful alien trio with Rystáll Sant and Lyn Me.

Jabba's palace on Tatooine is hidden away in the Western Dune Sea.

Suction-tipped fingers

Pheromone-suppressing bracelet

Antennae detect vibrations

Flamboyant hairstyle (only female Rodians have hair; males have head spikes)

Dancing costume

Singing for Hutts
Rystáll Sant, Greeata, and Lyn Me perform together at Jabba's palace. Graceful and rhythmic dancers make a powerful impression on the heavy, slow-moving Hutts. All the performers compete for Jabba's favor and indulgence.

Greeata's love of music
and dance began as a youngster on her home planet of Rodia. She started out playing the kloo horn, and took a job on board a luxury liner, where she met fellow singer Sy Snootles. Together they formed a performing duo, which Max Rebo spotted playing in a cantina.

DATA FILE
AFFILIATION: Jabba's entourage
HOMEWORLD: Rodia
SPECIES: Rodian
HEIGHT: 1.7 m (5 ft 7 in)
APPEARANCES: III, VI
SEE ALSO: Sy Snootles; Lyn Me; Rystáll; Max Rebo

GREEDO
RODIAN BOUNTY HUNTER

GREEDO IS A RODIAN bounty hunter who works for Jabba the Hutt. During the Clone Wars, he kidnaps Baron Papanoida's daughters, Che Amanwe and Chi Eekway. When Greedo demands debt payment from Han Solo in a Mos Eisley cantina, he finally meets his match.

Rodians like Greedo come from a culture that favors bounty hunting as a sport.

Head spikes

Large eyes see in infra-red spectrum

Well-worn flightsuit

Blaster pistol

Greedo's End

The confrontation that takes place in the crowded cantina between Greedo and Han Solo begins with Greedo pulling a blaster on Solo. When Solo claims not to have the money on him, there is an exchange of blaster fire—and the Rodian falls dead on the table. Solo leaves, tossing a few coins at the bartender to hush up the incident.

Long, dexterous fingers

DATA FILE

AFFILIATION: Bounty hunter
HOMEWORLD: Rodia
SPECIES: Rodian
HEIGHT: 1.73 m (5 ft 8 in)
APPEARANCES: IV, CW
SEE ALSO: Han Solo; Anakin Skywalker; Jabba the Hutt

Greedo grew up

on Tatooine and was known for his temper. He sometimes attempted to start fights with others, including Anakin Skywalker, who was then a slave in Mos Espa.

HAILFIRE DROID
MOBILE MISSILE LAUNCHERS

HAILFIRE DROIDS ROLL rapidly into action, firing murderous explosive missiles from launcher pods. Their large hoop wheels move the droids at an intimidating speed. A red photoreceptor "eye" locks onto both land and air targets at impressive distances, giving the droids great reach.

Hailfire droids, flanked by battle droids, roll toward the Republic Army on Geonosis.

Deadly Missiles

Hailfire droids have two racks of missile launchers on either side of their droid heads. Each rack carries 15 guided missile warheads. A single missile can destroy a gunship or AT-TE walker.

DATA FILE

AFFILIATION: Separatist
TYPE: Droid tank
MANUFACTURER:
  Haor Chall Engineering
HEIGHT: 8.5 m (27 ft 11 in)
APPEARANCES: II
SEE ALSO: Homing spider
  droid; dwarf spider droid

The powerful
InterGalactic Banking Clan donates its hailfire droids to the Separatist army. Before the war started, it used these droids to ensure its loans were paid back on time.

Photoreceptor

Hoop wheel

Missile rack

HAN SOLO

SMUGGLER TURNED REBEL HERO

HAN SOLO IS A pirate, smuggler, and mercenary. With his loyal first mate, Chewbacca, he flies one of the fastest ships in the galaxy—the *Millennium Falcon*. Han is reckless at times, but proves himself a natural leader in the Rebel Alliance.

Solo might be foolhardy, but he is courageous too—a match for any adventure!

Solo works his way from a poor childhood, through petty thievery, to a commission in the Imperial Academy. But he is expelled! When Solo wins the *Falcon* in a game of sabacc (a popular card game), he becomes master of his own destiny.

Customized blaster pistol

Corellian spacer black vest

Droid caller

Corellian blood stripe

Action boots

Strike Force

Han Solo leads a group of Rebels, including Chewbacca and Leia, in a risky mission on Endor's Moon to destroy the Imperial shield generator. Solo shows Princess Leia that there is more to being a scoundrel than having a chequered past!

DATA FILE

AFFILIATION:
Rebel Alliance
HOMEWORLD: Corellia
SPECIES: Human
HEIGHT: 1.8 m (5 ft 11 in)
APPEARANCES: IV, V, VI
SEE ALSO: Chewbacca;
Princess Leia

HOMING SPIDER DROID

SEPARATIST SPIDER WALKERS

THE COMMERCE GUILD'S CONTRIBUTION to the Separatist ground forces is the homing spider droid. It is an all-terrain weapon capable of precise targeting and sustained beam fire from its laser cannons. This metallic walking monster is a real danger to Republic walkers and gunships.

Homing spider droids patrol the lush vegetation of the Separatist stronghold on Felucia.

DATA FILE

AFFILIATION: Separatist
TYPE: Battle droid
MANUFACTURER:
Baktoid Armor
Workshop
HEIGHT: 7.32 m (24 ft)
APPEARANCES: II
SEE ALSO:
Dwarf spider droid

In Command

Homing spider droids move swiftly over battlefields on their long, powerful legs. The homing spider droid's main weapon is a top-mounted laser cannon, with a smaller, anti-personnel cannon positioned below it.

Extension hydraulics

Armored body core

Ambulation motors

Before the start of the Clone Wars, the Commerce Guild uses its homing spider droids to intimidate and control other large corporations, and to enforce tribute payments. At this time, armies are illegal, but many giant corporations flaunt huge security forces composed of deadly droids.

Parallax signal tracing dish

Homing laser

HOTH REBEL TROOPER

REBEL FOOT SOLDIERS

REBEL SOLDIERS ARE a rag-tag bunch. Some are deserters from the Imperial forces but many more are young volunteers with little or no experience in combat. New recruits receive basic training in handling weapons, communications, and emergency medical relief.

Rebel troops use tripod-mounted blasters at the Battle of Yavin.

Anti-glare goggles

Thermal flak jacket

Binoculars

Relocation

After the Battle of Yavin, the Alliance relocates its secret headquarters to Hoth. Anticipating an Imperial invasion, the Rebels modify their weapons to function in the icy temperatures.

Rebel troops on the ice planet Hoth must adapt quickly to freezing temperatures and the constant risk of sudden evacuation. They are equipped with specialist snow gear, including thermal flak jackets and polarized anti-glare goggles.

DATA FILE

AFFILIATION: Rebel Alliance

SPECIES: Human

STANDARD EQUIPMENT: Tripod-mounted blasters; thermal flak jackets; anti-glare goggles

APPEARANCES: IV, V, VI

SEE ALSO: Rebel trooper

IG-88
HIDEOUS ASSASSIN DROID

IG-88 IS A HEAVILY armed assassin droid who offers his services to Darth Vader to capture the *Millennium Falcon* after the Battle of Hoth. IG-88 is one of four identical droids which massacred their constructors moments after they were activated.

A wrecked IG-88 droid is left for scrap in Cloud City after Boba Fett caught it trailing him.

Heat sensor

Vocoder

DATA FILE

AFFILIATION: Bounty hunter

TYPE: Assassin droid

MANUFACTURER: Holowan Laboratories

HEIGHT: 1.96 m (6 ft 5 in)

APPEARANCES: V

SEE ALSO: Boba Fett; Darth Vader

Outlaws

IG-88 joins the motley assortment of human, alien, and droid bounty hunters on the deck of Vader's ship, the *Executor*. IG-88 and Boba Fett are long-time rivals. Assassin droids like IG-88 were outlawed after the Clone Wars, but they continue to stalk the galaxy.

Ammunition bandolier

Pulse cannon

IG-88 is obsessed with hunting and killing, as a result of its incompletely formed droid programming. The IG-series was designed to have blasters built-in to each arm, but they were never installed.

Acid-proof servo wires

IMPERIAL DIGNITARY

THE EMPEROR'S HIGH OFFICIALS

HIGH OFFICIALS form a society of sycophants and back-stabbers, who owe their posts to Emperor Palpatine's whim. While Palpatine rules the galaxy, these Imperial advisors manage the Empire and carry out the Emperor's will.

A group of the most powerful advisors form the Imperial Security Council.

Coruscanti headwear

DATA FILE

AFFILIATION: Empire
HOMEWORLD: Coruscant
SPECIES: Human
APPEARANCES: VI
SEE ALSO: Palpatine; Darth Vader

Crimson vest for show

Sleeves hide small blaster

Vastly expensive underlining

Ceremony

A small group of advisors accompany the Emperor to the second Death Star when Palpatine arrives to make his inspection of the superweapon's construction. He also puts into motion a ploy to destroy the Rebel Alliance once and for all.

Palpatine appoints Imperial advisors from many different worlds. Their duties include keeping a watchful eye on their home systems (and the systems of rival advisors) and performing administrative duties, such as the appointment of Imperial Governors and Moffs.

Lavish robe indicates high status

IMPERIAL DROIDS
THE EMPIRE'S UTILITY DROIDS

THE GALACTIC EMPIRE USES a range of droids with limited independence and zero personality. They are either existing droids adapted for Imperial purposes, or specialized new forms, including spy droids and illegal interrogator droids.

MSE (or "mouse") droids carry messages and lead troops on assigned posts.

Blaster cannon (under flap)

DATA FILE

AFFILIATION: Empire
TYPE: Droid
MANUFACTURER:
Industrial Automaton (R2-Q5)
HEIGHT: 96 cm (37 in)
APPEARANCE: IV, V, VI
SEE ALSO: Interrogator droid; Imperial probot

Spy Droid

Arakyd Industries produce RA-7 protocol droids specially for the Empire. Unlike most protocol droids, these have unpleasant personalities and are almost always used as spies.

Heat exhaust

Motorized leg

R2-Q5 is one of the many Imperial astromechs that patrol the corridors of the Death Star, doing maintenance and repair tasks. Many such droids are fitted with secret spy devices that allow human overseers to monitor personnel.

Powerbus cable for tread

IMPERIAL PROBOT

REBEL-SEEKING PROBE DROID

INTELLIGENT AND EERIE Imperial probots, also known as probe droids, relentlessly search the galaxy for any signs of the Rebel Alliance. They float above the ground on repulsorlifts and silenced thrusters. Probots are armed with blasters for self-defense and can self-destruct if captured.

Hyperdrive pods carry probots to their destination planets.

Transmiter dome

Holocam

DATA FILE

AFFILIATION: Empire
TYPE: Probe droid
MANUFACTURER: Arakyd Industries
HEIGHT: 1.6 m (5 ft 3 in)
APPEARANCES: V
SEE ALSO: Interrogator droid; Darth Vader

Invasion

A probot sent out from the Star Destroyer *Avenger* detects the Rebel base on Hoth, and sends its images of the power generators back to Darth Vader. The Dark Lord immediately prepares his Death Squadron for a full-scale invasion of the frozen planet.

Sampling claw

Reinforced joint

Manipulator limb

After the Battle of Yavin, when the Alliance destroys the Death Star, the Empire sends out thousands of probots into every corner of the galaxy to find the hidden Rebel bases. The probots use their sensors to discover a location's secrets and communicate their findings to distant Star Destroyers.

High torque limb

IMPERIAL RED GUARD
PALPATINE'S SECURITY FORCE

ROYAL, OR RED, GUARDS ARE Emperor Palpatine's personal bodyguards. From the time of his appointment to Supreme Chancellor, these Guards have accompanied Palpatine at all times.

Red Guards eventually come to replace the blue-robed guards of the Galactic Senate.

Full-face helmet with darkened visor

Long robe conceals hidden weapons

Force pike

Synthetic leather combat gloves

Confrontation
When Moff Jerjerrod and two Red Guards attempt to deny Darth Vader entrance to the Emperor's throne room on the second Death Star, Vader Force-chokes the officer, though not fatally.

Red Guards use vibro-active force pikes, which inflict precise and lethal wounds. Palpatine keeps the details of the Guards' training in deadly arts a secret, citing "security concerns."

DATA FILE

AFFILIATION: Republic/ Empire
HEIGHT: 1.83 m (6 ft)
APPEARANCES: II, III, VI
SEE ALSO: Palpatine; Darth Vader; Imperial Dignitary

INTERROGATOR DROID
IMPERIAL TORTURE DEVICE

WHEN PRINCESS LEIA REFUSES to discuss the location of the hidden Rebel base, Darth Vader brings in an interrogator droid or, more accurately, a torture droid. Illegal by the laws of the Republic, torture droids are technological horrors invented behind the curtains of Imperial secrecy.

Torture droids hover and spin on repulsors, while flexing their terrible pincers and needles.

Chemical torture turret

DATA FILE

AFFILIATION: Empire
TYPE: Interrogator droid
MANUFACTURER:
Imperial Department of Military Research
WIDTH: 30 cm (12 in)
APPEARANCES: IV
SEE ALSO: Princess Leia; Darth Vader

Undefeated

Princess Leia had hoped the rumors of such atrocities as interrogator droids were not true. Subjected to the machine's manipulations, Leia somehow maintains her resistance, even when she is near the point of death from the pain.

Drug injector

Hypnotic power strip

Interrogator droids
are completely without pity. They exploit every physical and mental point of weakness with flesh peelers, joint cripplers, bone fragmenters, electroshock nerve probes, and other unspeakable devices.

Victim pain response monitors

J'QUILLE
WHIPHID HUNTER

J'QUILLE IS A BRUTAL Whiphid from the frozen planet Toola. He works as a bounty hunter for Jabba the Hutt, though he is really a spy for a rival crime lord. He plans to kill the Hutt by poisoning his food.

Whiphids are huge, furred beings from the planet Toola. They have powerful tusks.

Retractable eyes

Coarse fur

J'Quille works for Jabba's main rival on Tatooine, Lady Valarian, a female Whiphid with whom J'Quille also had an affair. After he fails to kill Jabba, Lady Valarian places a large bounty on J'Quille's head. Unable to leave Tatooine, he joins the B'omarr monks.

DATA FILE

AFFILIATION:
Jabba's entourage
HOMEWORLD: Toola
SPECIES: Whiphid
HEIGHT: 2 m
(6 ft 7 in)
APPEARANCES: VI
SEE ALSO:
Jabba the Hutt;
Princess Leia

Survivor

J'Quille witnesses and survives the battle at the Great Pit of Carkoon. When Princess Leia strangles Jabba the Hutt, J'Quille's own murderous plans are foiled.

JABBA THE HUTT

NOTORIOUS CRIME LORD

THE REPELLENT CRIME LORD Jabba the Hutt commands an extensive criminal empire. He built his operation through a long history of deals, threats, extortion, deaths, and good business sense. Now Jabba lives a life of wickedness in his palace located in the remote desert of Tatooine.

Princess Leia extracts the revenge that all of Jabba's slaves have dreamed about.

Hutt skin secretes oil and mucus

Body has no skeleton

Ruler

Sitting on his throne, with his slaves and sycophants all around, Jabba presides over a court of murderous depravity. Many bounty hunters and hired thugs seek work here.

Muscular body can move like a snail

Jabba Desilijic Tiure, known to all as Jabba the Hutt, comes from the planet Nal Hutta, where he was raised by his father, Zorba the Hutt, also a crime lord. Hutts are notorious for their ruthless ways and run most of the galaxy's large criminal empires.

DATA FILE

AFFILIATION: Crime lord
HOMEWORLD: Nal Hutta
SPECIES: Hutt
LENGTH: 3.9 m (12 ft 10 in)
APPEARANCES: I, IV, VI, CW
SEE ALSO: Bib Fortuna;
Salacious Crumb

JAN DODONNA
REBEL COMMANDER ON YAVIN 4

GENERAL JAN DODONNA IS A master tactician for the Rebel Alliance. He commands the assault on the Death Star in the Battle of Yavin. Dodonna identifies the supposedly invulnerable station's single flaw: a small thermal exhaust port that leads straight to the explosive main reactor.

General Dodonna briefs the Rebel pilots in the command room at the Rebel base on Yavin 4.

DATA FILE

AFFILIATION: Rebel Alliance
HOMEWORLD: Commenor
SPECIES: Human
HEIGHT: 1.83 m (6 ft)
APPEARANCES: IV
SEE ALSO: Luke Skywalker; Princess Leia

Rebel command insignia

Rebel tactician's uniform

Commenor-style belt buckle

Ground Support

During the strike on the Death Star, Dodonna provides the Rebel pilots with ground support from Yavin. His strategy enables a fleet of 30 one-man fighters to destroy a battlestation over 160 kilometers (100 miles) wide.

Jan Dodonna

offers his skill and expertise to the Alliance once the Empire comes to power. After witnessing the role raw speed plays in the Battle of Yavin, he conceives of the A-wing starfighter design.

JANGO FETT
MANDALORIAN BOUNTY HUNTER

AFTER THE MURDER OF his parents, Jango Fett was raised by a group of legendary warriors, known as the Mandalorians. He becomes one of the best bounty hunters in the galaxy.

Fett in his ship *Slave I* blasts Obi-Wan Kenobi's Jedi starfighter in the Geonosis asteroid field.

WESTAR-34 blaster

Eye sensor allows Jango to see behind him

Segmented armor plate allows flexibility

Gauntlet projectile dart shooter

Lethal Opponent
In battle with Obi-Wan Kenobi, Fett launches himself into the air using his jetpack. He carries many weapons, including kneepad rocket launchers, wrist-mounted whipcord throwers, and wrist gauntlets that fire darts and blades.

DATA FILE
AFFILIATION: Bounty hunter
HOMEWORLD:
 Concord Dawn
SPECIES: Human
HEIGHT: 1.83 m (6 ft)
APPEARANCES: II
SEE ALSO: Boba Fett

Fett's reputation as a
supreme warrior led the Kaminoans to recruit him for their secret army project: every clone trooper is a clone of him. Fett wears the armored uniform that helped make the Mandalorians a dreaded name.

Segmented armor plate

JAR JAR BINKS
ROGUE GUNGAN TURNED SENATOR

JAR JAR BINKS is an amphibious Gungan from Naboo. In the invasion of Naboo, Jedi Qui-Gon Jinn runs into and rescues Jar Jar. Jar Jar becomes a general in the Gungan Grand Army, and then a Junior Representative in the Galactic Senate.

Clumsy General Jar Jar proves at first more of a hindrance than a help at the Battle of Naboo.

Haillu (earlobes) for display

DATA FILE

AFFILIATION: Republic
HOMEWORLD: Naboo
SPECIES: Gungan
HEIGHT: 1.96 m
(6 ft 5 in)
APPEARANCES:
I, II, III, CW
SEE ALSO:
Qui-Gon Jinn,
Padmé Amidala

Cast-off stretchy Gungan pants

Powerful calf muscles for swimming

Good Intentions

In Padmé's absence, Jar Jar represents Naboo in the Senate. With the best of intentions, Jar Jar sets in motion a new galactic era, as he proposes a motion for Supreme Chancellor Palpatine to accept emergency powers to deal with the Separatist threat.

Jar Jar is well-meaning but accident-prone. This simple soul is elevated to a position in the Senate that may be beyond his abilities. Luckily for him, the Naboo value purity of heart over other qualifications to govern.

Tight trouser ends keep out swamp crawlies

99

JAWA
ROBED METAL MERCHANTS

JAWAS SCAVENGE SCRAP metal, lost droids, and equipment on Tatooine. When Jawas arrive to sell and trade at the edge of town, droids stay away and individuals watch their landspeeders extra closely: Things tend to disappear when Jawas are around!

Most Jawas patrol the dunes and dusty rocks in gigantic sandcrawlers.

Glowing eyes

Heavy hoods protect from sun glare

Bandolier

Ionization blaster

Desert Find
Unlucky droids that wander off or get thrown out as junk are favorite targets for the Jawas. They carry any finds to their sandcrawlers, where a magnetic suction tube draws the captured droid into the bowels of these ancient mining vehicles.

Timid, greedy Jawas
wear dark robes to protect them from Tatooine's twin suns. Their glowing eyes help them see in the dark crevices where they hide, and their rodent-like faces are remarkably ugly to non-Jawas.

DATA FILE

AFFILIATION: Non-affiliated
HOMEWORLD: Tatooine
HEIGHT: 1 m (3 ft 3 in)
APPEARANCES: I, II, IV, VI, CW
SEE ALSO: Tusken Raider

JOCASTA NU
JEDI ARCHIVIST

MADAME JOCASTA NU is Director of the Jedi Archives in the Jedi Temple on Coruscant. Her astonishing memory seems to rival the Archives itself, which she runs as a tool rather than a service, expecting Jedi and support personnel to do their own research.

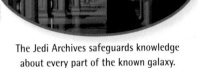

The Jedi Archives safeguards knowledge about every part of the known galaxy.

Traditional Ansata pattern symbolizing knowledge and learning

Proud Archivist

When Obi-Wan Kenobi cannot locate the planet Kamino in the Archives records, Jocasta Nu insists that then it cannot exist. Later, Jocasta discovers evidence that Count Dooku had sabotaged the records on Kamino to protect the secrecy of the building of the clone army.

DATA FILE

AFFILIATION: Jedi
HOMEWORLD: Coruscant
SPECIES: Human
HEIGHT: 1.67 m (5 ft 6 in)
APPEARANCES: II, CW
SEE ALSO: Obi-Wan Kenobi; Count Dooku

Pouch contains data storage crystals and hologlobes

Madame Nu trained as a Jedi before she ran the Jedi Archives. However, she chooses to pursue the path of knowledge, instead of seeking an active combat role. Nu travels the galaxy gathering data for the Archives. However, she retains a keen grasp of lightsaber combat.

Lightsaber still worn as testament of field service

KI-ADI-MUNDI

CEREAN JEDI MASTER

CEREAN JEDI MASTER Ki-Adi-Mundi has a high-domed head, which holds a complex binary brain. He becomes a Jedi General in the Clone Wars and fights on Geonosis and Mygeeto, among others.

Ki-Adi-Mundi had two teachers: the mysterious Dark Woman and Yoda.

Large brain supported by second heart

Cerean cuffs

Travel pouch

Into Battle

Ki-Adi-Mundi fights alongside Clone Commander Bacara in many battles, including the attack on Mygeeto. But when Order 66 is activated, the clone troops turn on him. He defends himself bravely, but is finally killed.

DATA FILE

AFFILIATION: Jedi
HOMEWORLD: Cerea
SPECIES: Cerean
HEIGHT: 1.98 m (6 ft 6 in)
APPEARANCES: I, II, III, CW
SEE ALSO: Commander Bacara; Yoda

Ki-Adi-Mundi sits on the Jedi Council. He is a thoughtful Jedi who shows great skill and courage in battle. Unusually for Jedi, Mundi is allowed to marry, since Cereans have an exceptionally low birth rate.

Cerean fighting boots

KIT FISTO
NAUTOLAN JEDI MASTER

JEDI MASTER KIT FISTO is a fierce fighter who joins the 200 Jedi Knights that travel to Geonosis to rescue the captives from the deadly Execution Arena. During the Clone Wars, Fisto accepts a seat on the Jedi High Council and is a veteran of many campaigns.

Kit Fisto leads a special unit of clone troopers at the Battle of Geonosis.

Low light-vision eyes

Tentacles detect chemical signatures of opponents

Jedi robe

DATA FILE

AFFILIATION: Jedi
HOMEWORLD: Glee Anselm
SPECIES: Nautolan
HEIGHT: 1.96 m (6 ft 5 in)
APPEARANCES: II, III, CW
SEE ALSO: Mace Windu

Fallen Jedi

Most Jedi are deployed on distant worlds, but Mace Windu manages to assemble a trio of celebrated swordsmiths, including Kit Fisto, to assist him in arresting Palpatine. However, few Jedi of Mace's generation have fought a Sith Lord, and the Jedi fall to Sidious's blade.

As an amphibious Nautolan from Glee Anselm, Kit Fisto can live in air or water. His head tentacles are highly sensitive and allow him to detect others' emotions. This ability allows Fisto to take instant advantage of an opponent's uncertainty in combat.

KO SAI

CHIEF SCIENTIST ON THE CLONE ARMY

KAMINOAN CHIEF SCIENTIST Ko Sai oversees the biological aspects of the clone army project. She supervises the delicate redesign of the clones' genetic codes to accelerate their growth to twice the normal human rate and make them highly obedient to authority.

Kamino's cities stand on stilts in Kamino's seas, forming colonies around the planet.

Serum sample pouch

Black body-glove underlayer

Black cuff is a mark of honor

Speed Learning

Ko Sai and her engineers developed special training helmets for the young clones, to enhance their learning ability. Despite her close involvement in their training, Ko Sai feels nothing for the clones, and quickly destroys any that she judges to be imperfect. Her outwardly polite manner masks her true intolerance of physical imperfection.

DATA FILE

AFFILIATION: Non-affiliated
HOMEWORLD: Kamino
SPECIES: Kaminoan
HEIGHT: 2.21 m (7 ft 3 in)
APPEARANCES: II
SEE ALSO: Lama Su;
 Obi-Wan Kenobi

White form-fitting clothing

In the Clone Wars, Ko Sai
disappears. Various groups want her found: the Republic must prevent her secrets falling into enemy hands, certain clones want the secret to a normal lifespan, and Palpatine seeks the genetic means to live forever.

Digitigrade configuration of feet adds height

LAMA SU
KAMINO'S PRIME MINISTER

LAMA SU IS PRIME MINISTER of Kamino, where the clone army is being created. He met with Sifo-Dyas, the mysterious Jedi who placed the order for a clone army. Lama is not concerned with the use of the army, only of the financial benefit for his people.

Kaminoans fly on aiwhas between their cities. Aiwhas can fly and swim with equal ease.

Elongated bones allow limited flexibility in neck

DATA FILE

AFFILIATION: Non-affiliated
HOMEWORLD: Kamino
SPECIES: Kaminoan
HEIGHT: 2.29 m (7 ft 6 in)
APPEARANCES: II
SEE ALSO: Ko Sai; Obi-Wan Kenobi

Grand Tour

Lama Su personally takes Obi-Wan Kenobi on a tour of the cloning facility. The Prime Minister is one of the few Kaminoans to have any contact with off-worlders. But he is still not entirely comfortable in their presence. He makes no mention of Kenobi's unfamiliarity with the project.

Cloak of office

Dexterous fingers

Kamino is a remote, watery planet, cut off from the larger arena of galactic events. Lama Su is only marginally interested in off-world politics, and thinks only of the technical challenges of cloning a mass army.

Small feet adapted to firm Kaminoan seabeds and now to hard flooring

LANDO CALRISSIAN
BARON ADMINISTRATOR OF CLOUD CITY

DASHING LANDO Calrissian is a rogue, con artist, smuggler, and gambler, who won control of Cloud City in a game of sabacc. He has come to enjoy his new-found sense of responsibility as Baron Administrator.

Lando disguises himself as a lowly skiff guard at Jabba's palace to aid in the rescue of Han Solo.

Tarelle sel-weave shirt

Borrowed Rebel blaster

Lando's Cloud City is a fabulous mining colony on Bespin. After leaving the city, Lando falls in with the Rebels. He is promoted to General and still finds adventure, but now contributes his abilities to a greater cause.

Royal emblems

DATA FILE

AFFILIATION: Rebel Alliance

HOMEWORLD: Unknown

SPECIES: Human

HEIGHT: 1.78 m (5 ft 10 in)

APPEARANCES: V, VI

SEE ALSO: Lobot; Han Solo; Ugnaught

Betrayed

Calrissian is forced to betray Han Solo and his friends to Darth Vader in order to preserve Cloud City's freedom. When he learns that the Sith Lord has no intention of keeping his side of the bargain, Lando plots a rescue mission and escapes from the city he once ruled.

LOBOT
CLOUD CITY'S CHIEF ADMINISTRATIVE AIDE

LOBOT IS CLOUD City's Chief Administrative Aide. He keeps in direct contact with the city's central computer via cybernetic implants that wrap round his head. Lobot can monitor a vast array of details at once.

Efficient and near-silent Lobot is the ideal assistant to flamboyant Lando Calrissian.

City central computer link

DATA FILE

AFFILIATION: Rebel Alliance
HOMEWORLD: Bespin
SPECIES: Human/Cyborg
HEIGHT: 1.75 m (5 ft 9 in)
APPEARANCES: V
SEE ALSO: Lando Calrissian

Belt projects clear-signal field

Fineweave sherculién-cloth shirt

To the Rescue

Lobot has no special love for Palpatine's Empire. When Lando Calrissian turns against Darth Vader and decides to rescue Han Solo's friends, Lobot's connection to the central computers proves useful. In response to Lando's "Code Force Seven," Lobot arrives with Cloud City guards to free Leia, Chewbacca, and C-3PO.

Lobot was a slaver's son, until pirates killed his father. Lobot escaped to Cloud City, where he was arrested for stealing. To repay his debt, he agreed to have a cybernetic headbank surgically fitted into his head, so he could serve the city. Even after his sentence ended, Lobot continued on in the role.

LOGRAY
EWOK HEAD SHAMAN

LOGRAY IS AN EWOK TRIBAL SHAMAN and medicine man. He uses his knowledge of ritual and magic to help and awe his people. The shaman still favors the old Ewok traditions of initiation and live sacrifice. After the Battle of Endor, Logray will be exposed as a fraud and cast out from the Ewok village.

Logray and Chief Chirpa eventually persuade their tribe to join the Rebels in their fight.

DATA FILE

AFFILIATION: Republic/ Rebel Alliance
HOMEWORLD: Endor
SPECIES: Ewok
HEIGHT: 1 m (3 ft 3 in)
APPEARANCES: VI
SEE ALSO: Chief Chirpa

Churi skull

Staff of power

Medicine bag

In his youth, Logray was a great warrior. His staff of power is adorned with trophies, including remnants of old enemies. Logray is suspicious of all outsiders, an attitude reinforced by the arrival of Imperial forces.

Striped fur

Honor Feast

Logray first decides that Han Solo, Luke Skywalker, Chewbacca, and R2-D2 will be sacrificed. They will be the main course at a banquet to honor C-3PO, who the Ewoks believe is "a golden god."

LUKE SKYWALKER

LEGENDARY REBEL PILOT AND JEDI

TATOOINE FARMHAND Luke Skywalker is thrown into a world of adventure when he discovers a secret message inside one of his new droids. Luke becomes a space pilot for the Rebel Alliance and fulfills his true destiny as a legendary Jedi Knight.

In close combat with Darth Vader, Luke discovers the truth about his father.

DATA FILE

AFFILIATION: Rebel Alliance
HOMEWORLD: Tatooine
SPECIES: Human
HEIGHT: 1.72 m (5 ft 8 in)
APPEARANCES: III, IV, V, VI
SEE ALSO: Princess Leia;
 Han Solo; Yoda; Darth Vader

Jedi Path

Luke first climbs into the cockpit of an X-wing in the attack on the first Death Star. Fighting for the Rebel Alliance in the years afterward, Luke becomes a great leader. Yoda helps to awaken Luke's Force abilities, and, as a Jedi, Luke faces the challenges of the Emperor and Vader, holding the galaxy's hope for freedom.

Tatooine farm tunic

Tool pouch

Droid caller

Anakin Skywalker's lightsaber

Young Luke Skywalker yearns

to escape the dull chores on his uncle's moisture farm. His only chance for excitement is flying his T-16 skyhopper— his piloting skills are excellent. Luke will return to Tatooine when he leads the rescue of Han Solo from Jabba the Hutt.

LUMINARA UNDULI
MIRIALAN JEDI MASTER

BORN ON THE COLD, DRY world of Mirial, Luminara Unduli joined the Jedi Order at a young age. She fights against Count Dooku's droid soldiers at the Battle of Geonosis and is one of the few Jedi to survive the onslaught. Unduli serves as a Jedi General in the Clone Wars.

Luminara Unduli will lose her life on Kashyyyk when Order 66 is signalled.

Mirialan facial tattoo

Battle on Geonosis

Luminara Unduli and more than 200 other Jedi fight Count Dooku's army of droids and Geonosian soldiers in the Geonosis arena. After a fierce battle, she is one of a handful of Jedi still standing when Jedi Master Yoda arrives with the newly created clone army to rescue them.

Form III lightsaber position

DATA FILE

AFFILIATION: Jedi
HOMEWORLD: Mirial
SPECIES: Mirialan
HEIGHT: 1.7 m (5 ft 7 in)
APPEARANCES: II, III, CW
SEE ALSO: Barriss Offee

Unduli is a Mirial Adept, a warrior who has perfected her combat skills. She has seen action in the Clone Wars on worlds such as Ilum, Nadiem, and Geonosis.

LYN ME

PERFORMER IN THE MAX REBO BAND

LYN ME IS A TWI'LEK DANCER and backup singer in the Max Rebo Band at Jabba's palace. She studied Twi'lek dance and quickly gained the attention of Max Rebo, who is constantly on the lookout for new talent.

Lyn travels the galaxy with the Max Rebo Band.

Lekku (head-tail)

Sensua bindings

Elegant hand position

Rescued

Boba Fett saved the young Lyn Me and many others from slavery. Her village elders had pooled their meager resources to pay the famed bounty hunter to exterminate the slavers. As a result, Lyn Me hero worships Fett. While dancing at Jabba's palace, she spots Boba Fett, and makes plans to talk to him.

Dance shoes

Lyn Me grew up on the barren northern continent of Ryloth, the Twi'leks' homeworld. Her species has suffered generations of hardships, with many Twi'leks being sold into slavery by the criminal underworld that exists in their culture.

DATA FILE

AFFILIATION: Jabba's entourage
HOMEWORLD: Ryloth
SPECIES: Twi'lek
HEIGHT: 1.6 m (5 ft 3 in)
APPEARANCES: VI
SEE ALSO: Rystáll; Greeata

MACE WINDU

LEGENDARY JEDI MASTER

MACE WINDU IS A SENIOR member of the Jedi High Council. His wisdom and combat prowess are legendary. Windu is somber and cool-minded, but he is also capable of dramatic actions in the face of danger.

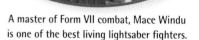

A master of Form VII combat, Mace Windu is one of the best living lightsaber fighters.

Coarseweave tunic

Well-known lightsaber with amethyst blade

DATA FILE

AFFILIATION: Jedi
HOMEWORLD: Haruun Kal
SPECIES: Human
HEIGHT: 1.88 m (6 ft 2 in)
APPEARANCES: I, II, III, CW
SEE ALSO: Yoda; Anakin
   Skywalker; Palpatine

Jedi utility belt

Gut Instinct

Mace Windu's suspicions about Chancellor Palpatine are proved right when Anakin reveals that Palpatine is a Sith Lord. Windu takes immediate action, promising to take Palpatine into Jedi custody, dead or alive.

Mace is decisive and perceptive. He is one of the first Jedi to sense danger in Anakin Skywalker and is quick to lead a Jedi taskforce to Geonosis when war preparations are discovered there.

Jedi boots offer excellent traction

Jedi tunic allows ease of movement in combat

MAGNAGUARD
GENERAL GRIEVOUS'S DROID BODYGUARDS

GENERAL GRIEVOUS'S BODYGUARDS are built to the alien cyborg's own specifications and trained by him. MagnaGuards often fight in pairs and can adjust their combat styles to match those of their opponents. They are equipped with deadly electrostaffs, or grenades and rocket launchers.

MagnaGuards use their electrostaffs to stun or kill opponents.

Mumuu cloak markings match those on Grievous's mask

Electrostaffs are resistant to lightsaber strikes

Cloak is combat-tattered

DATA FILE

AFFILIATION: Separatist
TYPE: Bodyguard droid
MANUFACTURER: Holowan Mechanicals
HEIGHT: 1.95 m (6 ft 5 in)
APPEARANCES: III, CW
SEE ALSO: General Grievous

MagnaGuards replicate the elite group of warriors and bodyguards that would always accompany Grievous when he was a Kaleesh warlord. Other Separatist leaders, including Count Dooku, come to use the MagnaGuards as bodyguards or soldiers.

Battle-scarred legs

Heel can extend for greater stability

Double Trouble

Anakin Skywalker and Obi-Wan Kenobi fight two MagnaGuards, IG-101 and IG-102, on Grievous's command ship *Invisible Hand*, when they attempt to rescue Palpatine. Even when Kenobi slices the head off one of the droids, it uses backup processors to continue fighting!

MALAKILI
KEEPER OF JABBA'S RANCOR

JABBA'S ANIMAL HANDLER, Malakili, takes care of a murderous rancor monster that Jabba keeps in a pit beneath one of his palace courts. Malakili has grown fond of the fearsome beast, and regards it as a kind-hearted creature and a friend!

Jabba's rancor once saved Malakili's life when Sand People attacked him.

Leather hood

Sweat-soaked rag belt

DATA FILE
AFFILIATION: Jabba's entourage
HOMEWORLD: Corellia
SPECIES: Human
HEIGHT: 1.72 m (5 ft 8 in)
APPEARANCES: VI
SEE ALSO: Rancor

Wrist guard

New Start
When Luke Skywalker kills the rancor, Malakili weeps openly. He had been planning to betray Jabba to the rival gang boss, Lady Valarian, and to leave with the rancor beast. After Jabba's death, Malakili teams up with the palace chef and opens a successful restaurant in Mos Eisley named the Crystal Moon.

Malakili once worked as an animal handler in a traveling circus. He became an outlaw when one of his dangerous circus beasts escaped during a show on Nar Shaddaa and killed members of the audience. After this incident, Malakili was sold to Jabba the Hutt.

Ancient circus pants

MAS AMEDDA
CHAGRIAN SENATE SPEAKER

MAS AMEDDA IS SPEAKER of the Galactic Senate on Coruscant where he keeps order in debates. Amedda is a stern and stoic Chagrian, and is one of a select few who understand that Palpatine is more than he appears to be.

Amedda is the first to suggest that the Senate should give Palpatine emergency powers.

Speaker's staff

Attack and display horns

Blue skin screens out harmful radiation

Standing Firm

Mas Amedda is by Palpatine's side after the fight with Yoda in the Senate, when Palpatine's personal shock troopers search for signs of the Jedi Master. Amedda continues to hold office as Palpatine transforms the Republic into the Galactic Empire.

During Valorum's term as Supreme Chancellor, Mas Amedda is Vice Chair of the Galactic Senate. Secretly working for Palpatine, Amedda does everything in his power to tie up the Senate in endless debates so that Valorum loses the support of many Senators.

Robes of state

DATA FILE

AFFILIATION: Republic/ Empire
HOMEWORLD: Champala
SPECIES: Chagrian
HEIGHT: 1.96 m (6 ft 5 in)
APPEARANCES: I, II, III, CW
SEE ALSO: Palpatine

MAX REBO

LEADER OF JABBA'S HOUSE BAND

THE BLUE ORTOLAN, KNOWN IN the entertainment business as Max Rebo, is a half-insane keyboard player who is completely obsessed with food. When the pleasure-loving crime boss Jabba the Hutt offers Max a contract that pays only in free meals, he immediately accepts—to the outrage of his bandmates!

Max Rebo's band accompanies Jabba's entourage on the Hutt's sail barge.

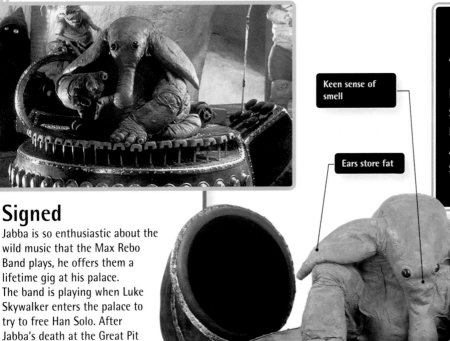

Keen sense of smell

Ears store fat

Air intake

Fingertips can absorb food and drink

DATA FILE

AFFILIATION: Jabba's entourage
HOMEWORLD: Orto
SPECIES: Ortolan
HEIGHT: 1.5 m (4 ft 11 in)
APPEARANCES: VI
SEE ALSO: Sy Snootles; Droopy McCool

Signed

Jabba is so enthusiastic about the wild music that the Max Rebo Band plays, he offers them a lifetime gig at his palace. The band is playing when Luke Skywalker enters the palace to try to free Han Solo. After Jabba's death at the Great Pit of Carkoon, the band breaks up.

Max Rebo's real name is Siiruulian Phantele. For a Ortolan, he is quite skinny. His obsession with food may lead him to have poor judgment as the leader of his band, but he is devoted to music and quite good at his chosen instrument—the red ball jet organ.

MOFF JERJERROD
SUPERVISOR OF THE SECOND DEATH STAR

MOFF JERJERROD SUPERVISES the construction of the second Death Star. During the Battle of Endor, Jerjerrod commands the station's superlaser against the Rebel forces. He is killed when the Rebels finally detonate the Death Star's reactor.

Jerjerrod blames slow progress of the Death Star's construction on a shortfall of workers.

Rank insignia plaque

Imperial code cylinder

Imperial officer's disc

Jerjerrod was born to a wealthy family on the Core World of Tinnel IV. He shows petty spitefulness and a lack of ambition as he rises through the Imperial ranks, both admirable qualities in a Moff. When he is assigned to the top-secret second Death Star project, his cover title is Director of Imperial Energy Systems.

Imperial officer's tunic

Called to Account

When the construction of the Death Star falls behind schedule, the Emperor sends Vader to put additional pressure on Moff Jerjerrod and his construction crews. Informed that the Emperor himself will soon be arriving, Jerjerrod assures Vader his men will double their efforts.

DATA FILE

AFFILIATION: Empire
HOMEWORLD: Tinnel IV
SPECIES: Human
HEIGHT: 1.7 m (5 ft 7 in)
APPEARANCES: VI
SEE ALSO: Darth Vader; Captain Needa

Naval boots

MON MOTHMA
REBEL ALLIANCE LEADER

MON MOTHMA IS THE highest leader of the Rebellion. As a member of the galactic Senate, she champions the cause of freedom until the Emperor's evil closes in around her. Abandoning the Senate, Mothma works with Bail Organa to form the Rebel Alliance that aims to unseat the Galactic Empire.

After the fall of the Empire, Mothma will become the New Republic's first Chief of State.

Hanna pendant

Simple Chandrilan hairstyle

DATA FILE

AFFILIATION: Republic/ Rebel Alliance
HOMEWORLD: Chandrila
SPECIES: Human
HEIGHT: 1.5 m (4 ft 11 in)
APPEARANCES: III, VI, CW
SEE ALSO: Bail Organa

Rebel Founders

Mon Mothma and Bail Organa become convinced that Palpatine needs to be opposed. With the Jedi Council and the Senate under his control, and his newly appointed governors overseeing all star systems, the two loyalists make a pact with a few dependable Senators to form a highly secret Rebellion movement.

Gesture of reconciliation

Shraa silk mantle

Elegant robe of Fleuréline weave

Mon Mothma was born into a political family and became the youngest Senator to enter the Senate. When the Republic collapses, she goes underground and begins to organize the various cells of resistance into a single unity: The Alliance to Restore the Republic (or Rebel Alliance).

MUFTAK

MOS EISLEY CANTINA PATRON

MUFTAK IS A TALZ PICKPOCKET who lives in abandoned tunnels beneath Mos Eisley. He is a regular in the booths of Chalmun's Cantina. He is drinking in the Cantina on the day that Obi-Wan Kenobi and Luke Skywalker arrive in search of a spacer who will agree to take them off-world.

Muftak's thick fur protects his species from the frozen climate of its homeworld.

Day vision eyes (night vision eyes beneath)

Criminal Activities

Muftak is friends with various Cantina regulars. When not drinking, he plans robberies with a Chadra-Fan female named Kabe. In a raid on Jabba the Hutt's townhouse in Mos Eisley, they escape with data relating to the Rebel Alliance, which they sell to the Empire in return for safe passage off-world.

Sharp talons

Proboscis for feeding and communicating

Talz are a primitive species from the planet Alzoc III (with a colony on Orto Plutonia) who use few tools. Muftak was abandoned in Mos Eisley as a newborn. He grew up knowing he was different to others, but he had no knowledge of his species or background.

DATA FILE

AFFILIATION: Non-affiliated
HOMEWORLD: Alzoc III
SPECIES: Talz
HEIGHT: 2.1 m (6 ft 11 in)
APPEARANCES: IV
SEE ALSO: Figrin D'an

MUSTAFARIAN
(NORTHERN)

NORTHERN MUSTAFARIANS ARE tall, thin aliens from the volcanic planet Mustafar. Two species of Mustafarians (Northern and Southern) evolved separately in underground caves. After the two species made contact with each other, they teamed up to collect valuable minerals from the lava flows.

Mustafarians prefer to ride lava fleas, even though they also have repulsorlift travel.

Equipment backpack

Mustafarians from the North have less resistance than the Southern species to the high temperatures of the lava streams, so they generally wear insulated armor and ride lava fleas.

Insulated armor

Secret Mine

As well as working directly on the lava flows, the Mustafarians operate a mining facility, which becomes a secret base for the leaders of the Separatist movement toward the end of the Clone Wars. Anakin Skywalker and Obi-Wan Kenobi fight their epic duel through the mine and to the lava streams beyond.

DATA FILE

AFFILIATION: Separatist
HOMEWORLD: Mustafar
SPECIES: Mustafarian
HEIGHT: 2.29 m (7 ft 6 in)
APPEARANCES: III
SEE ALSO: Mustafarian (Southern)

Shock-resistant exoskeleton

Eyes distinguish between light and darkness

Powerful legs for jumping

MUSTAFARIAN
(SOUTHERN)

SOUTHERN MUSTAFARIANS ARE stockier than their Northern counterparts, and their tough skin can resist higher temperatures. Southern Mustafarians have powerful bodies that can lift heavy equipment with relative ease. To work close to the lava flows, however, even they need to wear insulated armor.

Mustafar's hot climate and ash clouds have isolated the planet for most of its history.

DATA FILE

AFFILIATION: Separatist
HOMEWORLD: Mustafar
SPECIES: Mustafarian
HEIGHT: 1.5 m (4 ft 11 in)
APPEARANCES: III
SEE ALSO: Mustafarian (Northern)

Lava Miners

Mustafarian miners are known as lava skimmers for their job of dipping pole-mounted cauldrons (also called "lava skimmers") into the bubbling lava streams.

Breath mask

Armor recycled from discarded lava flea shells

Lava-resistant cauldron

The Mustafarians have had a trade agreement with the Techno Union for hundreds of years to supply it with minerals from the lava streams. The Techno Union provides them with droid lava collectors and repulsorlift harvesting platforms.

NABOO GUARD
BODYGUARD OF THE NABOO MONARCHY

THE NABOO ROYAL Guard is the highly trained bodyguard of the Naboo monarch and court. Its loyal, dedicated soldiers typically experience battle off-planet and return to Naboo to protect the royal house out of loyalty.

Naboo forces use small Gian landspeeders in their attempt to repel the invading droid army.

Blast-damping armor

Utility belt

Unarmored joints for agility

DATA FILE

AFFILIATION: Republic
HOMEWORLD: Naboo
SPECIES: Human
APPEARANCES: I, II, CW
SEE ALSO: Captain Panaka; Padmé Amidala

No leg armor for mobility

Returning Forces

When the Trade Federation droid army invades Naboo, the Royal Guard gets its first taste of true battle. But the sheer number of battle droids means a defeat for Naboo. Fortunately, Queen Amidala and Head of Security, Captain Panaka, escape and are able to return, with the Gungans, to put an end to the droid occupation.

The Royal Guard forms

one component of the Naboo Royal Security Forces. They work alongside the Security Guard, who comprise mainly sentries and patrolmen, and the Space Fighter Corps, who fly N-1 starfighters. The Head of Security oversees all divisions.

Shin protectors

NEXU

FANGED ARENA BEAST

A NEXU IS ONE OF THE savage beasts let loose on condemned prisoners in the Geonosian arenas, for the amusement of an enthusiastic crowd. The nexu is native to Cholganna, where it lives and hunts in cool forests. Its secondary eyes see in infrared wavelengths, allowing it to spy the heat signatures of warm-blooded prey.

The nexu seizes prey in its fanged mouth, then shakes or bites the creature to death.

DATA FILE

HOMEWORLD: Cholganna
LENGTH: 4.5 m (14 ft 9 in)
DIET: Carnivorous
HABITAT: Forest
APPEARANCES: II
SEE ALSO: Padmé Amidala
acklay; reek

Secondary eyes for heat vision

Quills erect in combat

Forked tail

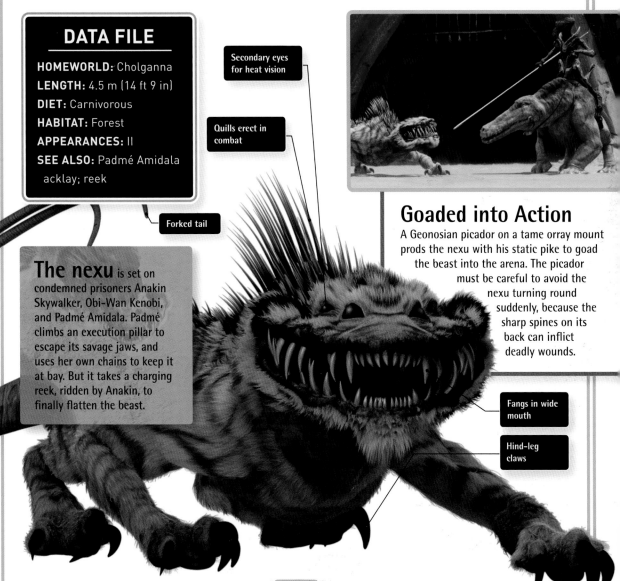

Goaded into Action

A Geonosian picador on a tame orray mount prods the nexu with his static pike to goad the beast into the arena. The picador must be careful to avoid the nexu turning round suddenly, because the sharp spines on its back can inflict deadly wounds.

The nexu is set on condemned prisoners Anakin Skywalker, Obi-Wan Kenobi, and Padmé Amidala. Padmé climbs an execution pillar to escape its savage jaws, and uses her own chains to keep it at bay. But it takes a charging reek, ridden by Anakin, to finally flatten the beast.

Fangs in wide mouth

Hind-leg claws

NIEN NUNB

COPILOT OF THE *MILLENNIUM FALCON*

NIEN NUNB IS Lando Calrissian's Sullustan copilot on board the *Millennium Falcon* at the Battle of Endor. Calrissian personally picked Nunb for the mission, as the two are old friends from their days as smugglers. Lando understands the Sullustan language that Nien speaks.

Nunb and Calrissian pilot the *Falcon* through the Death Star's unfinished superstructure.

Life support unit

DATA FILE

AFFILIATION: Rebel Alliance
HOMEWORLD: Sullust
SPECIES: Sullustan
HEIGHT: 1.6 m (5 ft 3 in)
APPEARANCES: VI
SEE ALSO: Lando Calrissian

Trusted Pilot

Nunb learned his piloting skills flying a freighter for the Sullustan SoroSuub Corporation. When SoroSuub began to support the Empire, Nunb showed his opposition by stealing from the company on behalf of the Rebel Alliance. At first, Nunb works independently, but he eventually becomes a full-time member of the Alliance.

Gear harness

Nien Nunb is one of

many Sullustans who serve as fighter pilots in the Rebel Alliance. His homeworld, Sullust, served as the staging area for the Rebel fleet before the Battle of Yavin. The Alliance awarded Nunb a medal named the Kalidor Crescent, for his bravery in the battle.

Insulated helmet

Pressurized g-suit

Energy-shielded fabric

NUTE GUNRAY

NEIMOIDIAN VICEROY

THE VICEROY OF THE Trade Federation, Nute Gunray, is powerful, deceitful, and willing to kill for his far-reaching commercial aims. Gunray becomes an unwitting pawn of Darth Sidious when he agrees to invade the peaceful planet of Naboo.

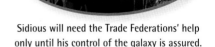

Sidious will need the Trade Federations' help only until his control of the galaxy is assured.

Viceroy's crested tiara

Nute Gunray is a Neimoidian, a species known for its exceptional greed. Gunray makes an alliance with Darth Sidious to blockade Naboo in opposition to increased taxation. However, Gunray feels increasingly uneasy when his alliance with Sidious leads to open warfare.

Wheedling expression

Viceroy's collar

True Face

Gunray's true cowardice shows itself when Padmé Amidala's freedom fighters storm the Royal Palace. Unable to hide behind battle droids any longer, Gunray is arrested. It is a sign of the Republic's decay that he is later able to buy his release and continue as Viceroy of the Trade Federation.

Long digits for counting profit

DATA FILE

AFFILIATION: Separatist
HOMEWORLD: Neimoidia
SPECIES: Neimoidian
HEIGHT: 1.91 m (6 ft 3 in)
APPEARANCES: I, II, III, CW
SEE ALSO: Rune Haako; Palpatine; Padmé Amidala

Elaborate Neimoidian clothing signifies wealth

OBI-WAN KENOBI

LEGENDARY JEDI MASTER

OBI-WAN KENOBI IS A TRULY great Jedi, who finds himself at the heart of galactic turmoil as the Republic unravels and finally collapses. Although cautious by nature, Kenobi has a healthy independent streak and truly formidable lightsaber skills.

Kenobi faces Darth Vader—once Kenobi's Padawan, Anakin Skywalker—in battle.

Under-tunic

Jedi robe

Kenobi's lightsaber skills are legendary

Kenobi's path is destined to lead in a very different direction to his Jedi partner, Anakin Skywalker's. After the Great Jedi Purge, Kenobi helps protect Luke and Leia Skywalker. For many years, he remains in hiding on Tatooine, watching over Luke Skywalker, the last hope for the ancient Jedi Order.

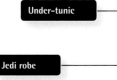

General Kenobi

Kenobi becomes a great Jedi General and pilot in the Clone Wars (despite being a reluctant flier!). Trained by the headstrong Qui-Gon Jinn, Kenobi trains his own master's protegé, Anakin Skywalker, after Jinn's death. The bond between Obi-Wan and Anakin is strong as they fight through the Clone Wars.

DATA FILE

AFFILIATION: Jedi
HOMEWORLD: Coruscant
SPECIES: Human
HEIGHT: 1.79 m (5 ft 10 in)
APPEARANCES: I, II, III, IV, V, VI, CW
SEE ALSO: Anakin Skywalker; Luke Skywalker

OCTUPTARRA DROID

TECHNO UNION BATTLE DROIDS

OCTUPTARRA DROIDS ARE TERRIFYING three-legged battle droids manufactured by the Techno Union. The droids have rotating laser turrets which can spin round to lock onto targets from any side in an instant. This makes them almost impossible for enemy troops to attack by surprise from behind.

After the establishment of the Empire, most octuptarra droids are deactivated.

DATA FILE

AFFILIATION: Separatist
TYPE: Battle droid
MANUFACTURER:
Techno Union
HEIGHT: 3.6 m (11 ft 10 in)
APPEARANCES: III, CW
SEE ALSO: Crab droid

Cognitive module and sensor suite

Rotating laser turret

Triple-jointed hydraulic limbs

Battle on Utapau

On Utapau, octuptarra droids protect General Grievous's headquarters from oncoming clone troopers. However, Clone Commander Cody's 212th Attack Batallion continues to push forward, at least until the initiation of Order 66 refocuses their priorities and they turn on the Jedi.

Octuptarra droids are named for the eight-eyed, gasbag-headed vine walkers found on Skako. The largest models are used as combat artillery, while agile battle droid-sized versions are used as antipersonnel weapons.

OOLA

TWI'LEK DANCER

OOLA IS A GREEN-SKINNED Twi'lek dancer enslaved to the cruel crime lord Jabba the Hutt. Jabba's major-domo, Bib Fortuna, kidnapped Oola from a primitive clan. He had other Twi'lek girls train Oola in the art of exotic dancing, so he could present her to his boss.

Oola dances for her life in Jabba's palace, but ends up in the dreadful rancor pit.

Lekku (head-tail)

Oola's life is tragic and short. Enslaved by Bib Fortuna, she has a chance to escape when Luke Skywalker meets her in Mos Eisley. However, Fortuna has fed her so many lies about the glory of Jabba's palace that she wants to see it for herself, so she refuses Luke's help.

Leather straps

Gruesome End

Jabba lavishes particular attention on Oola, keeping her chained to his throne. However, when Oola once more refuses Jabba's advances, the revolting Hutt is infuriated. He opens the trap door beneath the dance floor and watches as Oola is fed to his deadly rancor monster.

Flimsy net costume

DATA FILE

AFFILIATION: Jabba's entourage
HOMEWORLD: Ryloth
SPECIES: Twi'lek
HEIGHT: 1.6 m (5 ft 3 in)
APPEARANCES: VI
SEE ALSO: Jabba the Hutt

OOM-9
COMMAND OFFICER DROID

OOM-9 IS A BATTLE DROID commander who leads the droid army in the invasion of Naboo. His troops successfully capture the capital city of Theed and force the evacuation of the underwater Gungan city of Otoh Gunga.

OOM-9's first task as commander is to organize battle droids for the invasion of Naboo.

Macrobinoculars

Command officer markings

DATA FILE

AFFILIATION: Separatist
TYPE: OOM Command
  battle droid
MANUFACTURER: Baktoid
  Combat Automata
HEIGHT: 1.91 m (6 ft 3 in)
APPEARANCES: I
SEE ALSO: Battle droid

High-torque motors

OOM-9 was a standard B1 battle droid until he received special programming to serve as a command droid. He is fitted with antennae that allow him to communicate with the orbiting droid control ship.

Victory in Sight

On the verge of crushing the Gungan Grand Army on the Great Grass Plains, OOM-9 is stopped only when Anakin Skywalker destroys the Droid Control Ship.

Dried cartilage-shaped shin plates

Feet can be replaced with claws or pads

OPEE SEA KILLER

NABOO CREATURES OF THE DEEP

IN THE MURKY WATERS OF Naboo's underground lakes, a vicious creature lurks within dark caverns. The opee sea killer waits motionless, using a long, antenna-like lure on its head to attract the attention of its prey. It gives pursuit using its tail legs and jet propulsion vents to swim at great speed towards its prey.

The opee sea killer flicks out its long, sticky tongue to catch prey.

Lure

DATA FILE

HOMEWORLD: Naboo
LENGTH: 20 m (65 ft 7 in)
DIET: Carnivorous
HABITAT: Lakes, seas
APPEARANCES: I
SEE ALSO: Colo claw fish; sando aqua monster

Big Fish

The opee sea killer is smaller than some of the other predators in Naboo's lakes. So when it tries to grab a Gungan sub, carrying Jedi Qui-Gon Jinn and Obi-Wan Kenobi, and Gungan Jar Jar Binks, it unwittingly attracts the attention of the much larger sando aqua monster.

Opee sea killers are both aggressive and persistent. Even when attacked by large predators, they refuse to give up. Young opees have even been known to chew their way out of the belly of any creature that swallows them!

OPPO RANCISIS

JEDI HIGH COUNCIL MEMBER

OPPO RANCISIS IS A THISSPIASIAN Jedi Master who sits on the Jedi High Council. He joined the Jedi Order as an infant, and trained under Master Yaddle. When offered the throne of Thisspias, he declined it to continue to serve the galaxy as a Jedi. He is now a top Jedi military advisor.

Oppo uses the Jedi art of battle meditation to influence the outcome of a conflict.

Dense hair deters biting cygnats of Thisspias

DATA FILE

AFFILIATION: Jedi
HOMEWORLD: Thisspias
SPECIES: Thisspiasian
HEIGHT: 1.38 m (4 ft 6 in)
APPEARANCES: I, II
SEE ALSO: Yaddle

Second pair of hands hidden underneath cloak

Master Jedi

Rancisis is adept with his green-bladed lightsaber, but prefers to use his highly developed Force powers for combat. He is a formidable foe in unarmed combat, using his four arms and long tail to make surprising strikes at his opponent.

Fingers tipped with claws

Rancisis is an excellent strategist,

who ensures that, if negotiation fails, Jedi-counseled military tactics are cunning and effective. During the Clone Wars, Rancisis fights in the Siege of Saleucami, but also spends much time on Coruscant, coordinating Republic forces throughout the galaxy.

OWEN LARS
LUKE SKYWALKER'S GUARDIAN

AS A YOUNG NEWLYWED, Owen Lars made a huge decision. He agreed to hide and protect a newborn baby from the wrath of his own father: Darth Vader. The baby was named Luke by his mother, Padmé, moments before she died in childbirth. Owen gains a son, but also adds to his worries.

Owen, his wife Beru, and father Cliegg only once met Luke's parents, Anakin and Padmé.

Simple overcoat provides warmth in the cold desert evenings

Rough clothing made in Anchorhead

Young Owen
Lars was born to Cliegg Lars and his first wife Aika. He has spent most of his life on his father's farmstead on Tatooine, which he inherited after Cliegg passed away. Owen fell in love with Beru after meeting her in nearby Anchorhead. It is Beru who convinces the reluctant Owen to adopt Anakin's son.

Tunic

Tool pouch

A Farmer's Life
In later life, Owen and Luke work closely together on the family farmstead. They maintain the vaporators that collect precious moisture from the desert air, and buy "used" droids from passing Jawas. Although the teenage Luke is ready to fly the nest, Owen finds it hard to shrug off his gruff, protective attitude that has become a habit over the long years.

DATA FILE

AFFILIATION: Republic
HOMEWORLD: Tatooine
SPECIES: Human
HEIGHT: 1.7 m (5 ft 7 in)
APPEARANCES: II, III, IV
SEE ALSO: Beru Lars; Luke Skywalker; Cliegg Lars

Loose pants for desert climate

Sturdy boots

PADMÉ AMIDALA

NABOO QUEEN AND SENATOR

TIME AND AGAIN, PADMÉ AMIDALA has found
herself at the center of galactic events.
From the invasion of her home planet, Naboo,
to a death sentence in a Geonosian arena, by
way of multiple attempts on her life as a
Senator, Padmé faces extraordinary danger
with determination and great bravery.

Padmé and Anakin surrender to the love they
share, though they know it breaks Jedi rules.

DATA FILE

AFFILIATION: Republic
HOMEWORLD: Naboo
SPECIES: Human
HEIGHT: 1.65 m (5 ft 5 in)
APPEARANCES: I, II, III, CW
SEE ALSO: Anakin
  Skywalker; Captain Panaka

Armband signifies
political service

Slashes in clothing sustained
in Geonosian arena battle

Utility belt

Spare energy magazines
for blaster

Padmé grew up in a
small Naboo village. Exceptionally
talented, she was elected queen at
the age of only 14. At the end of
her term of office, Padmé is made
Senator of Naboo. It is on the
Galactic capital, Coruscant,
that she becomes closer to
Anakin Skywalker.

Queen turned Fighter

As the young Queen of Naboo, Padmé
Amidala has to learn that her cherished
values of non-violence will not save her
people from a brutal droid invasion.
Discarding her formal robes of state,
Padmé determines to inspire her own
troops to end the invasion by
capturing the Neimoidian leaders.

Light shin armor

Action boots
with firm grip

PALPATINE

SITH LORD AND GALACTIC EMPEROR

PALPATINE IS KNOWN by many names. First, he is
Senator Palpatine of Naboo. Then, he is Supreme
Chancellor Palpatine. Finally, he declares himself
Emperor and rules the galaxy. Ultimate power
has been his plan all along: Palpatine's
true name is Darth Sidious, the
most evil of Sith Lords.

As Palpatine, Sidious secretly plans the Clone
Wars to destroy the Republic and the Jedi Order.

Hood to hide
face

Palpatine manages to
keep all those around him from
suspecting his true identity.
For years, he has been patient
and unassuming, so few have
recognized his political
ambitions. His dark side
powers even blinded
the Jedi from seeing
behind his mask
of affability.

Sidious's true
identity is
known to few

Sith Powers

His face twisted and scarred by the
dark energies of the Force, Emperor
Palpatine is a figure of terrible power.
One of his most deadly weapons is Sith
lightning, which is projected from his
fingertips. A Force user can block the
lethal energy for a while if they are
strong, but it takes immense effort.

Black robe
hides Sidious
from sight

DATA FILE

AFFILIATION: Republic/
Empire

HOMEWORLD: Naboo

SPECIES: Human

HEIGHT: 1.78 m (5 ft 10 in)

APPEARANCES: I, II, III, V,
VI, CW

SEE ALSO: Darth Vader

PASSEL ARGENTE

MAGISTRATE OF THE CORPORATE ALLIANCE

PASSEL ARGENTE IS MAGISTRATE of the powerful Corporate Alliance. He has also served as Galactic Senator for his homeworld Kooriva. Argente commits the Corporate Alliance to military action to break up the Galactic Republic, and contributes his forces to the droid army.

Passel Argente hoped to play a minor role in the Clone Wars, but Sidious has other plans.

DATA FILE

AFFILIATION: Separatist
HOMEWORLD: Kooriva
SPECIES: Koorivar
HEIGHT: 1.86 m (6 ft 1 in)
APPEARANCES: I, II, III
SEE ALSO: Palpatine

Passel Argente is a Koorivar, a humanoid species with head horns, scales, and different-colored skin tones. As head of one of the galaxy's largest commercial corporations, Argente has become corrupted by his huge wealth and power. His aim in joining the Separatists is to become even wealthier!

Grasping hands

Robust male head horn

Koorivars have scaly, reptilian skin

Robe made of shimmerbird tongues

On Borrowed Time

Argente plots and schemes against his Separatist allies, spying on Wat Tambor and planning to overthrow Dooku. However, like all the Separatist leaders, he and his aide, Denaria Kee, are considered expendable when their usefulness to Emperor Palpatine, or Darth Sidious, ends.

PAU'AN WARRIOR
UTAPAU'S SECURITY FORCE

THE PEACEFUL PLANET of Utapau maintains a standing army of warriors to defend itself. All the city states across the planet contribute recruits to the Utapaun Security Force. The Security Force has been in hiding since the droid army occupied the planet and installed the Separatist leaders there.

Utapau's landing platforms, created from fossilized bones, stand empty during the occupation.

Exotic alloy helmet

Protective armor spikes

Shield design based on carapace of giant, burrowing turtles native to Utapau

Battle belt

Into Battle

After Jedi Knight Obi-Wan Kenobi confronts General Grievous on Utapau and summons the Republic Army, the Utapaun Security Force emerges from hiding. Pau'an warriors enter the battle against the occupying Separatists, some aboard flying reptiles named dactillions, while others reclaim their hidden starfighters and warships.

Pau'an warriors are armed with shields and vibro-blades (named bidents, with two blades). Troops are either trained to fly starfighters and other ships or to ride native creatures, such as flying dactillions and varactyl reptiles.

Vibro-bladed bident

DATA FILE

AFFILIATION: Republic
HOMEWORLD: Utapau
SPECIES: Pau'an
AVERAGE HEIGHT: 1.9 m (6 ft 3 in)
APPEARANCES: II, III
SEE ALSO: Tion Medon; Utai; Boga; Obi-Wan Kenobi

PILOT DROID
FA-SERIES DROIDS

DURING THE CLONE WARS and afterward, droid pilots are common in spaceships across the galaxy. The Trade Federation uses specially programmed battle droids as pilots, while other corporations, such as SoroSuub, manufacture non-armed models like FA-series pilot droids.

On Geonosis, FA-4 boards Dooku's ship to ready the craft for a speedy takeoff.

Fine-motor graspers

Extensible neck

Manipulator arm

DATA FILE

AFFILIATION: Droid
TYPE: Pilot droid
MANUFACTURER: SoroSuub Corporation
HEIGHT: 2.1 m (6 ft 11 in)
APPEARANCES: II, III, CW
SEE ALSO: Count Dooku

Logic processor module

High-torque shoulder motor

FA-4 is a wheeled pilot droid manufactured by the SoroSuub Corporation. On Coruscant and other developed planets, pilot droids often work in partnership with FA-5 valet droids, which escort passengers to and from SoroSuub airspeeders.

Power axis

Heavy-duty treads

Dooku's Pilot Droid

The aristocratic Separatist leader, Count Dooku, flies around the galaxy in a Punworcca 116-class interstellar sloop. He prefers to let a custom-programmed FA-4 pilot droid do the flying for him. This allows the Count time to plan ahead and plot his next moves.

PIT DROID

DROID PODRACER MECHANICS

BUSY, SLIGHTLY CLUMSY pit droids work in pit hangars and race arenas on planets where the high-speed sport of Podracing takes place. Pit droids assist with all Podrace maintenance tasks and report to human Podracer mechanics, who oversee complex decisions and custom engine modifications.

Jar Jar Binks finds out that pit droids pop open when tapped on the head.

Head plate protects against falling tools

Monocular photoreceptor

Hardened alloy casing

Illegal frequency jammer

Pit Droid Mishap

In the Boonta Eve Classic Podrace on Tatooine, Ody Mandrell is one of the crowd's favored pilots—young, daring, and with a powerful Podracer that causes plenty of damage to other craft in the race. That is until he pulls over to a pit stop and a pit droid is sucked right through his massive engine. Now he is out of the race!

Power wrench

DATA FILE

AFFILIATION: Droid
TYPE: Pit droid
MANUFACTURER: Serv-O-Droid
HEIGHT: 1.19 m (3 ft 11 in)
APPEARANCES: I
SEE ALSO: Podracers

Pit droids are programmed to take orders and carry them out as quickly as possible, without asking questions. Accordingly, their logic processors are quite basic. However, this can leave them confused about how to get a job done, causing mayhem in the process.

PLO KOON

JEDI HIGH COUNCIL MEMBER

PLO KOON IS A MEMBER of the Jedi High Council and a Jedi General in the Clone Wars. Koon is one of the most powerful Jedi ever, with awesome fighting abilities, strong telekinetic powers, and superb piloting skills. He also discovered the young Jedi, Ahsoka Tano.

Plo Koon's starfighter crashes into a city on the Neimoidian planet of Cato Neimoidia.

Finger talons

Thick hide covers body

Antiox mask

Loose Jedi cloak

Tragic Mission

At the end of the Clone Wars, Plo Koon leads a starfighter patrol above Cato Neimoidia. Without warning, his own clone troops begin firing at his ship. Order 66 had been given, causing all the pre-programmed clones to turn on their Jedi leaders. Plo's ship crashes into the planet and Koon is killed.

Plo Koon is a Kel Dor from Dorin. He wears a special mask to protect his sensitive eyes and nostrils from the oxygen-rich atmosphere of planets such as Coruscant. Koon fights in the Battle of Geonosis and many more conflicts in the Clone Wars.

Practical combat/ flight boots

DATA FILE

AFFILIATION: Jedi
HOMEWORLD: Dorin
SPECIES: Kel Dor
HEIGHT: 1.88 m (6 ft 2 in)
APPEARANCES: I, II, III, CW
SEE ALSO: Qui-Gon Jinn; Ki-Adi-Mundi

PODRACERS
ALIEN OUTLAW PILOTS

PODRACING IS NOT A sport for the faint-hearted! Podracers race at upward of 800 kilometers per hour (500 mph). No wonder it is a sport suited to the lightning reflexes and body mutations of alien species. In fact, the only unusual sight on the circuit would be a human pilot!

The 18 Podracers of Tatooine's famous Boonta Eve Classic line up on the starting grid.

Three eye stalks

Fancy crash suit mimics armor to impress crowds and other Podracers

Two stomachs proudly encased in armor plate

Wrist guard

DATA FILE

AFFILIATION: Non-affiliated
HOMEWORLD: Hok
SPECIES: Gran
HEIGHT: 1.22 m (4 ft)
APPEARANCES: I
SEE ALSO: Sebulba; pit droid; Anakin Skywalker

Born to Race

Podracer pilots come in all shapes and sizes. It is not unusual to see 24-fingered Xexto pilots like Gasgano or Dug pilots like Sebulba, who stand on their "arms" (front limbs). Gasgano's extra fingers allow him to operate multiple controls at once, while Xamsters like Neva Kee have adapted brains that process sensory data at high speed.

Mawhonic is a typical
Podracer from the Outer Rim. He lives outside the laws of the Republic, buying and selling spare parts to Hutts but refusing official Republic currency. His triocular vision comes in handy for split-second timing in races.

Armor vents prevent overheating

POGGLE THE LESSER
GEONOSIAN ARCHDUKE

THE ARCHDUKE OF GEONOSIS, Poggle the Lesser, rules the Stalgasin hive colony, which controls all the other major hive colonies on Geonosis. His factories build innumerable battle droids for the Separatists, using the labor of legions of downtrodden drones.

Commissioned to design a superweapon, Poggle hands the plans to Count Dooku.

Long wattles

High-caste wings

Aristocratic adornments

DATA FILE

AFFILIATION: Separatist
HOMEWORLD: Geonosis
SPECIES: Geonosian
HEIGHT: 1.83 m (6 ft)
APPEARANCES: II, III
SEE ALSO: Geonosian
soldier; Count Dooku

Command staff

Poggle emerged from a lower caste through the sheer force of his iron will to become Archduke. His power is assured by the income generated from the droid project. Yet Poggle does not foresee that his end will come when Sidious no longer needs his services.

Presiding Leaders

Poggle the Lesser presides over the first meeting of the Separatist leadership on his planet, as well as the trial of Anakin Skywalker, Obi-Wan Kenobi, and Padmé Amidala, who are accused of spying. Poggle and the other Separatists take refuge in the underlevels when Republic forces arrive.

POLIS MASSAN
TELEPATHIC KALLIDAHIN

THE PEACEFUL, silent aliens who inhabit Polis Massa are known as Polis Massans, but in fact are Kallidahin from Kallidah. They have become known as Polis Massans because they have spent so long on this rocky planetoid in the Outer Rim.

Polis Massa is a large rock that was once part of a planet that blew apart in a violent cataclysm.

Diagnostic fingertips

DATA FILE

AFFILIATION: Republic
HOMEWORLD: Kallidah
SPECIES: Kallidahin
HEIGHT: 1.4 m (4 ft 8 in)
APPEARANCES: III
SEE ALSO: Padmé Amidala

Remote control

Sample containers

Urgent Delivery

Yoda and Bail Organa flee to remote Polis Massa to escape Order 66. They are joined by Obi-Wan Kenobi, C-3PO, R2-D2, and Padmé Amidala, who is injured and about to give birth. Polis Massans and medical droids urgently work together to deliver Padmé's twins, Luke and Leia, but they cannot save Padmé herself.

Polis Massans are archaeologists and exobiologists who borrow some of the Kaminoans' cloning techniques to attempt to recreate life from tissues recovered from archaeological digs. They have been excavating Polis Massa, seeking remains of the extinct Eellayin civilization that they believe was ancestor to the Kallidahin.

Knee pads

PONDA BABA

AQUALISH THUG

PONDA BABA IS A thuggish Aqualish who tried to pick a fight with Luke Skywalker. Luke had entered a notorious Mos Eisley cantina with Obi-Wan Kenobi looking for a ride off-planet. However, he has made a mistake picking on the companion of a Jedi.

Teak Sidbam is a fellow Aqualish who is sometimes mistaken for Ponda Baba.

Facial tusks grow with age

Large eyes for seeing underwater on native planet

Stump left by severing of arm

DATA FILE

AFFILIATION: Non-affiliated
HOMEWORLD: Ando
SPECIES: Aqualish
HEIGHT: 1.7 m (5 ft 7 in)
APPEARANCES: IV
SEE ALSO: Doctor Evazan; Obi-Wan Kenobi

Ponda Baba teamed up with troublemaker Dr Evazan after saving his life and realizing that together they could make more money shipping spice for Jabba the Hutt. After the fight in the cantina, Evazan tries to use his medical training to reattach Ponda Baba's arm but fails, nearly killing the Aqualish in the process.

Cantina Confrontation

Ponda Baba and his partner-in-crime, Dr Evazan, are caught unprepared for an old man's ability with a lightsaber, an almost forgotten relic of the glory days of the Galactic Republic. But for Luke, too, this first demonstration of Kenobi's abilities with the weapon is a revelation, and a hint of the possible return of the Jedi.

POWER DROID

MOBILE POWER UNITS

SOME DROIDS ARE MADE FOR greatness, like sophisticated pilot or surgeon droids; others, like C-3PO, have greatness thrust upon them. But some droids are so commonplace, they are destined never to be noticed. Power droids, which function as mobile power generators, are such droids.

Power droids have very simple artificial intelligence, so they tend to get lost easily.

Power plugs

Power droids, either the EG-series, made by Veril Line Systems, or the GNK-series, made by Industrial Automaton, are sometimes named "gonk" droids because of the low honking noise they emit whilst operating. Industrial Automaton also made a tibanna gas-holding PLNK-series power droid in the Clone Wars.

Monochromatic photoreceptor

GNK Power Droids

In less-developed backwaters all around the galaxy, wherever there is a junk shop or a mechanic garage, it is likely there will be GNK power droids somewhere in the background. Watto's Junkshop on Tatooine has a few battered GNK units. Watto gives rundown merchandise a quick power-up to get a better price from customers.

Internal power generator

Droid feet

DATA FILE

AFFILIATION: Droid
TYPE: Power droid
MANUFACTURERS:
Industrial Automaton and Veril Line Systems
APPROX. HEIGHT: 1 m (3 ft 3 in)
APPEARANCES: I, IV, V, VI, CW
SEE ALSO: Pilot droid; 2-1B; C-3PO

PRINCESS LEIA

SENATOR AND REBEL LEADER

AS SENATOR FOR Alderaan, Princess Leia Organa makes diplomatic missions across the galaxy on her ship, the *Tantive IV*. Secretly, she works for the Rebel Alliance, making connections and obtaining much needed equipment.

On Endor, Leia proves that she is still one of the best shots in the Alliance.

DATA FILE

AFFILIATION: Rebel Alliance
HOMEWORLD: Alderaan
SPECIES: Human
HEIGHT: 1.5 m (4 ft 11 in)
APPEARANCES: III, IV, V, VI
SEE ALSO: Bail Organa;
   Luke Skywalker; Han Solo

Elaborate hairstyle is Leia's tribute to her mother, Padmé

Stolen Imperial blaster

Traditional gown worn by Alderaanian royalty

Raised on Alderaan by her adoptive father, Bail Organa, Leia has been well prepared for her royal position. She uses her high-placed connections wherever she can to aid the Alliance. Leia feels the weight of her responsibilities and chooses to hide her personal feelings. However, she is not immune to the charms of a dashing rogue captain. But it is not until Leia is exposed as a Rebel, that she feels able to be more herself.

Decisive Leader

Leia is a key command figure in the Rebel Alliance, overseeing important missions and planning strategy, alongside General Rieekan and other Alliance leaders. In Echo Base on Hoth, Leia peers intently at the scanners, alert to any signs of Imperial detection.

Travel boots

QUEEN APAILANA

PADMÉ AMIDALA'S SUCCESSOR

QUEEN APAILANA IS ELECTED queen of Naboo when she is just 12 years old, making her one of the youngest monarchs in the planet's history. After Order 66, Apailana harbors Jedi fugitives on Naboo, which leads to her assassination by the Empire.

Thousands follow Padmé Amidala's funeral procession through Theed.

Fan headdress worn in tribute to Padmé Amidala

White makeup is ancient Naboo royal custom

Though young, Apailana has what the Naboo look for in their rulers: purity of heart and an absolute dedication to the peaceful values of the planet. After Apailana's death, the Empire installs a puppet monarch—Queen Kylantha.

Veda pearl suspensas

Cerlin capelet

Standing Strong

Queen Apailana is one of the chief mourners at Padmé Amidala's funeral on Naboo. Padmé had supported Apailana's bid for election. Although the official explanation for Padmé's death is that she died at the hands of renegade Jedi, Apailana privately believes otherwise, and continues to support the Jedi.

Chersilk mourning robe

DATA FILE

AFFILIATION: Republic
HOMEWORLD: Naboo
SPECIES: Human
HEIGHT: 1.57 m (5 ft 2 in)
APPEARANCES: III
SEE ALSO: Padmé Amidala

QUI-GON JINN

JEDI WHO DISCOVERS "THE CHOSEN ONE"

QUI-GON JINN IS AN experienced but headstrong Jedi. He was Padawan to Count Dooku and teacher to Obi-Wan Kenobi. Jinn has sometimes clashed with the Jedi High Council over his favoring of risk and action: As a result, Jinn has not been offered a seat on the Council.

Qui-Gon Jinn is one of the few Jedi to have battled a Sith Lord—Darth Maul.

Jinn is a master of Form IV lightsaber combat

Long hair worn back to keep vision clear

DATA FILE

AFFILIATION: Jedi
HOMEWORLD: Unknown
SPECIES: Human
HEIGHT: 1.93 m (6 ft 4 in)
APPEARANCES: I, CW
SEE ALSO: Anakin Skywalker

Jedi tunic

The Chosen One

When Jinn encounters young Anakin Skywalker, he strongly believes he has discovered the prophesied individual who will bring balance to the Force. Seeking to free Anakin from slavery, Jinn bets Anakin's owner Watto for his freedom in a Podrace. The risk pays off, and Qui-Gon takes the boy to Coruscant to present him to the Jedi High Council, with mixed results.

Qui-Gon Jinn fights actively for the Galactic Republic, but he is struck down by the unruly dark energies of Darth Maul. After his death, Jinn becomes the first Jedi to live on in the Force, a gift he will pass on to Obi-Wan Kenobi, Yoda, and Anakin Skywalker.

"Jedi ready" stance

Rugged travel boots

R2-D2

THE BRAVEST DROID IN THE GALAXY

R2-D2 IS NO ORDINARY ASTROMECH droid. His long history of adventures has given him a distinct personality. He is stubborn and inventive, and is strongly motivated to succeed at any given task. Although R2-D2 speaks only in electronic beeps and whistles, he usually manages to make his point!

R2-D2 has many hidden tricks, including extension arms and rocket boosters.

DATA FILE

AFFILIATION: Droid
TYPE: Astromech droid
MANUFACTURER: Industrial Automaton
HEIGHT: 96 cm (3 ft 2 in)
APPEARANCES: I, II, III, IV, V, VI, CW
SEE ALSO: C-3PO; Princess Leia; Bail Organa

R2-D2 first distinguishes himself on board Queen Amidala's Royal Starship. He serves Anakin Skywalker during the Clone Wars and then Luke Skywalker during the Rebellion, flying in the droid socket of their spaceships.

Holographic projector

Power recharge coupler

Motorized, all-terrain treads

Risky Mission

At the end of the Clone Wars, R2-D2 is assigned to Bail Organa's diplomatic fleet. Princess Leia entrusts R2-D2 with the stolen Death Star plans and her urgent message to Obi-Wan Kenobi. He risks all kinds of damage to accomplish his mission.

Retractable third leg

R4-G9

OBI-WAN KENOBI'S ASTROMECH DROID

R4-G9 IS A BRONZE-DOMED astromech droid that is stationed at the Jedi Temple on Coruscant. She is briefly assigned to Obi-Wan Kenobi when he begins flying a new class of starfighter, while his regular droid, R4-P17, is adapted to fit the new ship. Kenobi uses R4-G9 again on his crucial mission to Utapau.

One of R4-G9's tasks is to transmit coordinates to the starfighter's hyperspace docking ring.

DATA FILE

AFFILIATION: Droid
TYPE: Astromech droid
MANUFACTURER: Industrial Automaton
HEIGHT: 96 cm (3 ft 2 in)
APPEARANCES: III
SEE ALSO: Obi-Wan Kenobi; R4-P17

Reader socket for data cards

Primary system ventilation port

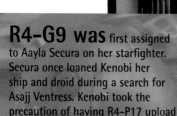

R4-G9 was first assigned to Aayla Secura on her starfighter. Secura once loaned Kenobi her ship and droid during a search for Asajj Ventress. Kenobi took the precaution of having R4-P17 upload his flight history records to R4-G9.

Tactics

Kenobi uses R4-G9 on Utapau after his own R4-P17 unit is destroyed in the Battle of Coruscant. In a diversionary tactic, G9 pilots Kenobi's ship off the planet alone and returns to the Republic Star Destroyer *Vigilance*, while Obi-Wan remains to track down General Grievous.

High-power coupling for system recharge

Power cables for mobility control

Housing holds main drive motor

R4-P17

OBI-WAN KENOBI'S ASTROMECH DROID

R4-P17 IS OBI-WAN KENOBI'S trusty astromech droid, used in his red starfighter. Before the Clone Wars, she was copilot when Kenobi chased Jango Fett through the asteroid rings above Geonosis. During the Clone Wars, R4-P17 took part in the Battle of Teth and many other conflicts, until her final destruction.

A buzz droid slices off R4-P17's domed head in the Battle of Coruscant.

Onboard logic function displays

Standardized body

Tools behind panels

Repurposed

Before the Clone Wars, R4-P17 had a specially modified body, which fitted into the narrow wing of Kenobi's starfighter. She was later repurposed and now has a full astromech body so she can fit into the latest models of starfighters.

R4 units

usually have conical heads, but R4-P17's head was crushed in an accident. Anakin Skywalker rebuilt her with a domed R2 head.

Treaded drives

R5-D4

ASTROMECH DROID SET TO DESTRUCT

R5-D4, ALSO KNOWN AS "Red," is a white and red astromech droid that Jawas on Tatooine sold to Owen Lars. However, immediately after the sale, Red's motivator blew up, and Owen returned him to the Jawas. This gives C-3PO the opportunity he needs to recommend that Owen takes R2-D2 instead.

R5-D4 will later become an intelligence gathering droid for the Rebel Alliance.

DATA FILE

AFFILIATION: Droid
TYPE: Astromech droid
MANUFACTURER: Industrial Automaton
HEIGHT: 97 cm (3 ft 2 in)
APPEARANCES: II, IV
SEE ALSO: R2-D2; Owen Lars; Jawa

Photoreceptor

Systems linkage and repair arms (under panels)

Sabotage

What Owen and Luke do not know is that R2-D2 sabotaged R5-D4 when they were inside the Jawas' sandcrawler. Usually, droids' programming forbids them to mess with other droids, but Leia instructs R2 to complete his mission at any cost.

R5-series droids are designed as cut-price versions of the superior R5 units. They are prone to defects and bad attitudes.

Recharge coupling

Third tread for balance over uneven surfaces

RANCOR

JABBA'S RAVENOUS PET

FEARSOME RANCOR MONSTERS are more than five meters (16 ft) tall, with thick skin and enormous strength. One specimen lives in a pit below Jabba the Hutt's throne room. The slimy, depraved gangster likes nothing more than to watch the rancor attack any unfortunate victims he chooses to cast into the pit.

Luke Skywalker prepares to battle for his life in Jabba's rancor pit.

DATA FILE

HOMEWORLD: Dathomir
HEIGHT: 5-19 m
(16 ft 5 in—63 ft 4 in)
DIET: Carnivorous
APPEARANCES: VI
SEE ALSO: Jabba the Hutt;
Bib Fortuna; Malakili

Armored skin can deflect laser bolts

Weak eyesight

Razor-sharp teeth

Hungry Beast

Jabba can operate a secret trap door located in front of his throne, which leads directly to his pet rancor below. When Luke Skywalker is thrown down, a Gamorrean guard falls with him and is then crushed in the rancor's jaws.

Rancors come from a remote planet named Dathomir. Most people think that rancors are entirely savage but in fact they have a primitive intelligence. Jabba's major-domo, Bib Fortuna, presented a rancor to Jabba as a birthday gift.

152

RAPPERTUNIE

MAX REBO BAND MEMBER

RAPPERTUNIE PLAYS A combination flute, or Growdi Harmonique, in Max Rebo's Band. Rappertunie has always had a thirst for travel and has used his musical talent to pay his way around the galaxy. Unfortunately, he ends up in a lifetime gig at Jabba's palace, where the hot, dry climate does not suit his moist skin at all.

Rappertunie plays away at the rear of the stage while secretly plotting his escape.

Rappertunie is the stage name of Rapotwanalantonee Tivtotolon. He is a Shawda Ubb— a small amphibious species with long fingers. Rappertunie was born on the swampy, wet Outer Rim planet, Manpha.

Moist skin

Long arms

Growdi

Defense

At Jabba's palace, Rappertunie can spend whole days perched motionless on his growdi seat, trying to keep his naturally moist skin cool. Being so small, Rappertunie has learned to spit paralyzing poison at any individuals who threaten him.

DATA FILE

AFFILIATION: Jabba's entourage
HOMEWORLD: Manpha
SPECIES: Shawda Ubb
HEIGHT: 30 cm (12 in)
APPEARANCES: VI
SEE ALSO: Max Rebo

REBEL TROOPER
GROUND FORCES OF THE REBEL ALLIANCE

REBEL SOLDIERS ARE the main forces of the Alliance to Restore the Republic. These dedicated troops are organized into Sector Forces, each of which is responsible for resisting the might of the Empire in their home sectors across the galaxy.

Fleet troopers on the *Tantive IV* wear a uniform of blue shirts, black combat vests, and gray pants.

Lightweight combat helmet

Rebel troops wear standardized uniforms wherever the Alliance's meager resources allow. SpecForce wilderness fighters—soldiers trained for specialized roles in Alliance Special Forces—wear full forest-camouflaged fatigues during the Battle of Endor.

Camouflaged cargo pants

High-resistance gloves

Commandos

Alliance SpecForce wilderness fighters infiltrate an Imperial base on Endor's forest moon. Under the command of General Solo, they manage to trick the squadrons of Imperial troops inside the base to come out, where they are outnumbered and forced to surrender.

Heavy-duty boots

DATA FILE

AFFILIATION: Rebel Alliance
SPECIES: Human
STANDARD EQUIPMENT:
 Blaster pistol
APPEARANCES: IV, V, VI
SEE ALSO: General Madine

REEK

GEONOSIAN ARENA BEAST

IN THE BRUTAL AND BLOODY arenas on Geonosis, reeks are one of the ferocious species kept for the purposes of execution and sport. Up against the mighty beast, Anakin Skywalker manages to use his Force powers to tame the reek enough to ride it, rather than letting it kill him.

Anakin gets the better of the arena reek, which Jango Fett later kills.

DATA FILE

HOMEWORLD: Ylesia
HEIGHT: 2.24 m (7 ft 4 in)
DIET: Omnivorous
HABITAT: Grassland
APPEARANCES: II, CW
SEE ALSO: Nexu; acklay

Red coloration produced by unnatural meat diet

Reeks are naturally herbivorous animals from the Codian Moon. They are cruelly starved into eating meat to provide entertainment in the arenas.

Combat

Reeks are slow-moving and heavy. However, they are dangerous fighters, with powerful jaws and horns that can gore opponents. In the wild, these horns are used for combat with other reeks.

Horn-teeth grow continuously

Sprawling posture makes reek relatively slow-moving

Cheek horns for dominance-combat headlocks

RUNE HAAKO
TRADE FEDERATION CHIEF ATTACHÉ

RUNE HAAKO IS A MEAN, greedy Neimoidian who provides diplomatic and legal advice to Viceroy Nute Gunray of the Trade Federation. He and Gunray are behind the invasion of Naboo.

Darth Sidious gives Haako and Gunray their orders via holoprojector to invade Naboo.

Skin mottled from self-indulgence

Attorney's cowl

Permanent scowl

Haako is nervous and pessimistic, often warning Nute Gunray of the risks of their alliance with Darth Sidious. When trouble brews, Haako's instinct is to either send in droidekas or flee.

Long, grasping fingers

Sumptuous robe

Coward

Rune Haako witnesses the start of the Clone Wars on Geonosis, and then helps direct the Separatist campaigns of the war from various safe hiding places. He and Nute Gunray move with the other Separatist leaders to the little-known Outer Rim planet Mustafar. This is where Rune will end his days when Darth Vader arrives with instructions to kill them all. Haako's final words are to beg for his life: "Stop! No!".

DATA FILE

AFFILIATION: Separatist
HOMEWORLD: Neimoidia
SPECIES: Neimoidian
HEIGHT: 1.96 m (6 ft 5 in)
APPEARANCES: I, II, III
SEE ALSO: Nute Gunray; Palpatine

Expensive cloth

RYSTÁLL

PERFORMER IN THE MAX REBO BAND

RYSTÁLL SANT'S ADOPTIVE parents are Ortolan musicians from Coruscant. They arrange for their dazzling daughter to perform as a singer and dancer with Max Rebo's band, where she will turn heads.

Rystáll and fellow singer Greeata are shocked by the depravities they witness at Jabba's palace.

Prominent head horns are sign of great beauty

Natural markings highlighted with stage makeup

Cape is a gift from a passing admirer, Syrh Rhoams

Rystáll is part human and part Theelin. The Theelin are a rare species with head horns, brightly colored hair, and mottled skin. Rystáll also has hooved feet. Many Theelin have artistic personalities and choose to become artists or performers.

Star Attraction

The colorful Rystáll Sant has always attracted the attention of a variety of characters, including the high-placed lieutenant in the criminal Black Sun organization, who tricked her into slavery. Lando Calrissian later freed her. At Jabba's palace she attracts the attention of bounty hunter Boba Fett.

Dancer's graceful body

Hooves

SABÉ

ROYAL NABOO HANDMAIDEN

SABÉ IS THE MOST IMPORTANT handmaiden in Queen Amidala's entourage. She is first in line to become the royal decoy in times of danger. Sabé dresses as the Queen and disguises her features with white makeup.

Sabé leads the delegation to ask the Gungans to join the Naboo in the fight for their planet.

Scar of remembrance

Royal headdress

Surcoat

Broad waistband

Queen Amidala's

handmaidens assist with many tasks necessary to maintain the monarch's regal image. These capable individuals are also trained in bodyguard skills and are equipped with pistols to defend their monarch in the event of a disturbance or emergency.

Royal Service

While Sabé is disguised as the Queen, Padmé Amidala dresses in the simple gown of a handmaiden. They use silent gestures and expressions to communicate secretly with each other. Sabé is trained to imitate the Queen in every way, but the task is a risky one.

DATA FILE

AFFILIATION: Republic
HOMEWORLD: Naboo
SPECIES: Human
HEIGHT: 1.65 (5 ft 5 in)
APPEARANCES: I
SEE ALSO: Padmé Amidala

Long battle dress made of blast-damping fabric

SAELT-MARAE

YARKORA INFORMANT

SAELT-MARAE, ALSO KNOWN as Yak Face, is one of the shady characters who hangs out at Jabba the Hutt's palace on Tatooine. He is an informant to both the Empire and the Rebels, whose particular skills are in coaxing secrets out of others without them even knowing it.

Saelt-Marae is a Yarkora—a secretive, long-lived species from the Outer Rim.

DATA FILE

AFFILIATION: Jabba's entourage

HOMEWORLD: Unknown

SPECIES: Yarkora

HEIGHT: 2.2 m (7 ft 2 in)

APPEARANCES: VI

SEE ALSO: Jabba the Hutt

Large ears for overhearing secrets

Highly sensitive whiskers

Three-fingered hand

Jabba the Hutt pays
Saelt-Marae to inform him of any goings-on in his palace that he might need to know about. In this way, Jabba learns about all the plots and schemes going on around him.

Informant

At Jabba's palace, Saelt-Marae poses as a trader. He chats away to anyone he meets, befriending them while secretly learning all their secrets, which he then passes on to Jabba. After Jabba's death beside the Sarlacc pit, Saelt-Marae steals his financial records and goes into hiding.

SAESEE TIIN

IKTOTCHI JEDI MASTER

JEDI MASTER SAESEE TIIN sits on the High Council in the Jedi Temple on Coruscant. His particular skills are in piloting the finest spacecraft at high speeds, which is also when his telepathic mind does its most focused thinking.

Tiin is one of the Jedi who confront Palpatine, now revealed to be Sidious.

DATA FILE

AFFILIATION: Jedi
HOMEWORLD: Iktotch
SPECIES: Iktotchi
HEIGHT: 1.88 m (6 ft 2 in)
APPEARANCES: I, II, III
SEE ALSO: Mace Windu

Well-developed horns

Tough skin protects against high winds of Iktotchon

Lightsaber

Customary humanoid Jedi robes

Jedi Fighter

Saesee Tiin fights at the Battle of Geonosis, riding on a Republic gunship to attack the droids on the plains. Later in the battle, Tiin takes to the skies to aid Jedi Master Adi Gallia in the battle above Geonosis. Tiin becomes a General in the Clone Wars, leading starfighter squadrons.

Saesee Tiin was born on Iktotch, the moon of Iktotchon. He flew starfighters from a young age and soon attracted the attention of Jedi scouts. Tiin trained under a unique master, Omo Bouri, who spoke only in energy pulses. After Bouri's death, Tiin became gravely inward looking, speaking only rarely.

SALACIOUS CRUMB

KOWAKIAN MONKEY-LIZARD

SALACIOUS CRUMB is Jabba the Hutt's court jester. When Jabba first found this Kowakian monkey-lizard stealing his food, the Hutt tried to eat him. Crumb escaped but Bib Fortuna captured him.

Crumb often irritates guests by repeating whatever Jabba says.

Highly senstive ears

Collar of scruffy fur

Hooked reptilian beak

Spindly arm

Salacious Crumb was just one of the many vermin on a space station, until he managed to stow away on board one of Jabba's spaceships, ending up on Tatooine. Now Crumb sits beside Jabba the Hutt, teasing all the inhabitants of the palace.

In Jest

Salacious Crumb knows that he must make Jabba laugh at least once a day, otherwise he will be killed. Crumb picks on everyone around him, in particular Jabba's new translator droid, C-3PO, who loses an eye to the hateful little creature.

Sharp talons

DATA FILE

AFFILIATION: Jabba's entourage
HOMEWORLD: Kowak
SPECIES: Kowakian monkey-lizard
HEIGHT: 70 cm (2 ft 3 in)
APPEARANCES: VI
SEE ALSO: Jabba the Hutt

SAN HILL

INTERGALACTIC BANKING CLAN CHAIRMAN

SAN HILL IS CHAIRMAN of the InterGalactic Banking Clan, one of the powerful financial bodies that funds and arms Count Dooku's Separatist movement. San is responsible for the rebuilding of General Grievous as a cyborg.

San Hill is the second biggest donor of troops to the droid army.

Muuns have three hearts, promoting long lifespans

Traditional financier's jacket

San Hill is a tall, thin Muun from the InterGalactic Banking world of Muunilinst. San is only ever able to view any situation in monetary terms, always calculating what profit he can make.

Body glove worn for fear of contamination from other species

Elongated fingers for counting profit

Debt

San Hill recruited Grievous when he was a Kaleesh warlord, making him a commander of the droid armies. To ensure permanent loyalty, San arranged for a bomb to be planted in Grievous's ship, nearly killing the general. The rebuilt cyborg now owes his life to Hill.

Height gives sense of superiority

DATA FILE

AFFILIATION: Separatist
HOMEWORLD: Muunilinst
SPECIES: Muun
HEIGHT: 1.91 m (6 ft 3 in)
APPEARANCES: II, III
SEE ALSO: Count Dooku; General Grievous

SANDO AQUA MONSTER

NABOO SEA CREATURES

THE FABLED SANDO aqua monster is a rarely seen beast in Naboo's oceans and lakes, despite its monstrous size. This creature swims using its long powerful tail and massive flippers. It also has clawed hands, which it uses to grasp prey. Male sando aqua monsters can grow up to 200 meters (650 ft) in length.

The people of Naboo tell many myths and legends about the feared sando aqua monster.

DATA FILE

HOMEWORLD: Naboo
LENGTH: 200 m (650 ft)
DIET: Carnivorous
HABITAT: Oceans, lakes
APPEARANCES: I
SEE ALSO: Opee sea killer

Muscular body

Flippers for swimming

Sea Monster

A sando aqua monster appears suddenly from the depths when Qui-Gon Jinn, Obi-Wan Kenobi, and Jar Jar Binks navigate the underground waters in a Gungan sub. They only escape when the opee sea killer pursuing the craft distracts the monster.

Webbed claws allow the creature to grab its prey

Sharp teeth

Little is known about the habits and evolution of sando aqua monsters. It is thought that they may have once lived on land. Some inhabitants of Naboo even claim to have seen them climbing out of the waters to attack land animals.

SANDTROOPER

DESERT-READY STORMTROOPERS

SANDTROOPERS ARE SPECIALIZED Imperial stormtroopers, trained to adapt to desert environments. They are equipped with armor and equipment for use in hot, dry climates. Their armor uses advanced cooling systems and their helmets have built-in polarized lenses to reduce sun glare.

Sandtroopers on Tatooine search for two droids carrying stolen Death Star plans.

Anti-sun glare lenses

Comlink system

Pauldron indicates rank

Sandtroopers police unruly planets such as Tatooine. They carry blaster rifles, long-range comlinks, plus food and water supplies. Sandtroopers' training enables them to adapt to local customs, like riding native dewback lizards on Tatooine.

Utility belt

Ranks

Sandtroopers wear shoulder pauldrons, which indicate rank. Regular sandtroopers' pauldrons are black, while sergeants wear white pauldrons. Squad leaders, who lead units of seven troopers, wear orange pauldrons.

DATA FILE

AFFILIATION: Empire

SPECIES: Human

HEIGHT: 1.83 m (6 ft)

STANDARD EQUIPMENT:
Blaster pistol; blaster rifle; repeating blaster

APPEARANCES: IV

SEE ALSO: Stormtrooper

SARLACC

LETHAL SAND-DWELLING LIFE-FORMS

IT IS FORTUNATE THE SARLACCS are so rare in the galaxy, since they are so utterly unpleasant. These monstrous life-forms hide beneath desert sands with their mouths just below the surface. Unwary individuals can easily find themselves slipping beneath the dunes into the waiting jaws of the terrifying creature.

The beaked tongue that rises from the Sarlacc's toothed mouth can swallow prey whole.

DATA FILE

HOMEWORLD: Tatooine
WIDTH: 3 m (9 ft 10 in)
DIET: Omnivorous
HABITAT: Desert
APPEARANCES: VI
SEE ALSO: Boba Fett

Inward-pointing teeth prevent victims from escaping

Touch-receptor tentacles

Captured Prey

Jabba intends to watch the Sarlacc feasting on Luke Skywalker and his friends. The creature does indeed feast on many bodies that day, but the Rebels manage to escape its jaws, and make a daring escape. Boba Fett is swallowed, but later manages to blast his way out of the Sarlacc's stomach.

The monstrous Sarlacc, which rests in the basin of the Great Pit of Carkoon in the Northern Dune Sea on Tatooine, is a favorite means for Jabba to dispose of any individuals who have particularly displeased him.

SCOUT TROOPER

SPECIALIZED STORMTROOPERS

IMPERIAL SCOUT TROOPERS are trained for long-term missions. They wear armor on the head and upper body only, to allow maximum maneuverability. Their helmets have enhanced macrobinocular viewplates, for precision target identification.

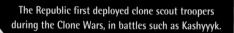

The Republic first deployed clone scout troopers during the Clone Wars, in battles such as Kashyyyk.

DATA FILE

AFFILIATION: Empire
SPECIES: Human
STANDARD EQUIPMENT:
 Blaster pistol; grenades;
 survival rations and gear
APPEARANCES: VI
 SEE ALSO: stormtrooper;
 sandtrooper

Survival rations

Body glove

On Patrol

Scout troopers on speeder bikes patrol the dense forests of Endor, where the Empire maintains a strategic shield generator. Working in units of two or four, they watch for any signs of troublesome forest creatures or terrorist infiltrators.

Scout troopers are sent to survey areas and locate enemy positions, infiltrate enemy territory, and undertake sabotage missions. They rarely engage in combat, and are instructed to call in stormtroopers at any signs of trouble.

Pistol holder

SEBULBA

STAR PODRACER

SEBULBA IS ONE of the top Podracers in the Outer Rim circuits. He is skilled at piloting his vehicle, but also willing to engage in dirty tricks to give him the winning edge. When Anakin Skywalker joins a race, he decides the young human must not win.

Sebulba pilots a giant, orange Podracer with many secret weapons concealed in it.

Grasping hands

Race goggles

Beaded danglers

Sebulba is a Dug from Malastare, a species notorious for being bullies. Playing up to his tough, violent image with the crowds, Sebulba wears a flashy, custom-designed leather racing suit.

Leather wrist guard

Reckless Driver

The dastardly Dug gives himself the winning edge in races by sabotaging other racers. Sebulba can pull up alongside another Podracer and blast it with his hidden flame thrower, or throw concussion weapons into another pilot's cockpit.

Trophy coins

DATA FILE

AFFILIATION: Podracer
HOMEWORLD: Malastare
SPECIES: Dug
HEIGHT: 1.12 m (3 ft 12 in)
APPEARANCES: I
SEE ALSO: Podracers

Tight leather leg-straps

SECURITY DROID

ARMED BATTLE DROIDS

SECURITY DROIDS WITH red markings are programmed for defense on spaceships, space stations, or buildings. These specialized droids work in squads led by a command officer battle droid (with yellow markings), such as OOM-9.

Security droids on board *Invisible Hand* are about to become scrap metal.

Optical sensor

Arm extension piston

Droid type designation markings

Security droids use standard E-5 blaster rifles. However, their programming is only a little more complex than regular battle droids, so they frequently miss their targets.

High-torque motors

E-5 blaster rifle

Droid Assault

Security droids patrol many Trade Federation capital ships. At the start of the blockade of Naboo, Jedi Qui-Gon Jinn and Obi-Wan Kenobi board the Trade Federation flagship to begin negotiations, and instead have to defend themselves from security droids. During the Clone Wars, Anakin and Obi-Wan face many security droids when they rescue Chancellor Palpatine from General Grievous's flagship, *Invisible Hand*.

DATA FILE

AFFILIATION: Separatist
TYPE: Battle droid
MANUFACTURER: Baktoid Combat Automata
HEIGHT: 1.91 m (6 ft 3 in)
APPEARANCES: I, II, III, CW
SEE ALSO: Battle droid; OOM-9

SEI TARIA is Chancellor Valorum's administrative aide. Taria helps Valorum with the plan to tax the outlying regions, an action that prompts the Trade Federation to blockade Naboo in protest—and ultimately starts the Clone Wars.

Sei Taria stands by Chancellor Valorum during Queen Amidala's vote of no confidence.

High Coruscanti collar

Sei Taria is close to Supreme Chancellor Valorum, and accompanies him on many diplomatic missions. There are even rumors of an affair. However, Taria also becomes close to Senator Palpatine, sensing his increasing power.

Septsilk robe signifies wealth

DATA FILE

AFFILIATION: Republic
HOMEWORLD: Spira
SPECIES: Human
HEIGHT: 1.78 m (5 ft 10 in)
APPEARANCES: I
SEE ALSO: Chancellor Valorum; Sly Moore

Standing Down

Queen Amidala's vote of no confidence removes Valorum from office, and ushers in Palpatine's term as Supreme Chancellor. Sei Taria leaves political life when Valorum does. It is rumored that blackmail threats from Palpatine's new aide, Sly Moore, force her departure.

SHAAK TI
TOGRUTA JEDI MASTER

JEDI MASTER SHAAK TI joined the Jedi High Council during the Clone Wars, when she also became an effective Jedi general. Ti escapes Darth Vader's massacre at the Jedi Temple, and organizes resistance to the Empire until Darth Vader's apprentice, Starkiller, defeats her.

Shaak Ti is the same species as Anakin Skywalker's apprentice, Ahsoka Tano.

Characteristic pigmentation of the Togruta species

Hollow montrals sense space

Two-handed grip for control

DATA FILE

AFFILIATION: Jedi
HOMEWORLD: Shili
SPECIES: Togruta
HEIGHT: 1.78 m (5 ft 10 in)
APPEARANCES: II, III, CW
SEE ALSO: Luminara Unduli

Jedi robe

Master Jedi

Ti fights alongside the other 200 Jedi Knights that come to the aid of Anakin Skywalker, Obi-Wan Kenobi, and Padmé Amidala on Geonosis. After the conflict in the arena, she boards a Republic gunship for the frontlines of the battle against the massed droid army.

As a Togruta, Shaak Ti is
one of the best Jedi fighters in group combat. Her hollow head montrals sense space ultrasonically, sharpening her spatial awareness. Where others struggle with the complexity of movements, Shaak Ti darts with ease.

SHMI SKYWALKER

ANAKIN SKYWALKER'S MOTHER

SHMI SKYWALKER HAS LIVED a hard life as a slave since pirates captured her parents when she was a girl. Owned by junk dealer Watto on Tatooine, Shmi gave birth to a child, whom she named Anakin and who also worked as a slave.

Shmi refuses to let her love for Anakin keep him from what she felt was his destiny—to be a Jedi.

Simple hairstyle typical of servants

DATA FILE

AFFILIATION: Republic
HOMEWORLD: Tatooine
SPECIES: Human
HEIGHT: 1.63 m (5 ft 4 in)
APPEARANCES: I, II
SEE ALSO: Cliegg Lars; Anakin Skywalker; Watto

Decorative belt

In spite of her poverty, Shmi tries to give Anakin a good home in the slave quarter of Mos Espa. Anakin's departure is hard for Shmi to bear, but she comes to live a happier life when a settler farmer, Cliegg Lars, frees her in order to marry her.

Tragic Loss

When Anakin Skywalker senses that his mother is in terrible pain, he travels to Tatooine to help her. However, he cannot prevent her death at the hands of the Sand People. Experiencing great anger and pain, Anakin vows to build his power until nothing can withstand it.

Simple skirt

Rough-spun tunic withstands harsh Tatooine weather

SHOCK TROOPER

MEMBERS OF THE CORUSCANT GUARD

AS THE REPUBLIC PREPARES FOR war, red-emblazoned shock troopers begin to patrol public spaces on Coruscant, to ensure public order and security. They also serve as bodyguards for politicians, including Supreme Chancellor Palpatine.

In the last days of the Republic, people begin to refer to shock troopers as stormtroopers.

Upgraded breath filter and annunciator

Coruscant designation

Shock-absorbing plastoid armor

Shock troopers are members of the Coruscant Guard. Palpatine set up the unit to strengthen the Coruscant Security Force and the Senate Guard. Shock troopers keep watch on government buildings and landing platforms.

DC-15 rifle

Stock holds power-charge magazine

Palpatine's Guard

Shock troopers go with Palpatine to the Senate after the Jedi's failed attempt to arrest him. They also unsuccessfully search for Yoda's body after his battle with Palpatine. Shock troopers also accompany Palpatine to Mustafar, where they find Darth Vader's burned body.

DATA FILE

AFFILIATION: Republic/ Empire
HOMEWORLD: Kamino
SPECIES: Human
HEIGHT: 1.83 m (6 ft)
APPEARANCES: II, III, CW
SEE ALSO: Stormtrooper

SHU MAI

PRESIDENT OF THE COMMERCE GUILD

SHU MAI IS PRESIDENT OF the powerful Commerce Guild, whose forces fight the Republic during the Clone Wars. Mai is a member of the Separatist Council alongside Nute Gunray, Wat Tambor, San Hill, and others. She is obsessed with status and power.

Shu Mai awaits her fate on volcanic Mustafar with the rest of the Separatist leaders.

DATA FILE

AFFILIATION: Separatist
HOMEWORLD: Castell
SPECIES: Gossam
HEIGHT: 1.65 m (5 ft 4 in)
APPEARANCES: II, III
SEE ALSO: Nute Gunray;
Wat Tambor; San Hill;
Count Dooku

Neck rings

Emblazoned jewel crest

Rich skirt made of rare uris silk

Shu Mai is a Gossam from the planet Castell. She is only concerned with status, power, and wealth. Mai worked her way up the Commerce Guild using aggressive and unscrupulous tactics, until no rivals stood in her way to becoming President.

Sneaky Practices

Shu Mai is the only Separatist leader to pledge her support to Dooku in secret, knowing that it amounts to treason. Though the Commerce Guild didn't openly back the Separatists, Shu Mai's homing spider droids began to fight on the battlefields of the Clone Wars.

Gossams have three-toed feet

SIO BIBBLE
GOVERNOR OF NABOO

SIO BIBBLE IS GOVERNOR of Naboo during the Trade Federation invasion. He oversees all matters brought to Queen Amidala's attention. He also chairs the Advisory Council, the governing body of Naboo. Sio is completely opposed to violence.

Bibble refuses to accept Captain Panaka's warnings of greater need for armament.

Formal collar

Fashionable Naboo sleeves and cuffs

DATA FILE

AFFILIATION: Republic
HOMEWORLD: Naboo
SPECIES: Human
HEIGHT: 1.7 m (5 ft 7 in)
APPEARANCES: I, II, III
SEE ALSO: Captain Panaka; Nute Gunray; Padmé Amidala

Philosopher's tunic

Under Arrest

During the invasion of Naboo, battle droids arrest Sio Bibble and Queen Amidala. When two Jedi Knights rescue Amidala, the governor chooses to stay with his people. Bibble leads them in a hunger strike, and earns the ire of the Trade Federation Viceroy, Nute Gunray.

Bibble is a philosopher who was elected governor under Amidala's predecessor, King Veruna. Sio is initially critical of Amidala, but comes to respect her. He later serves under Amidala's successors—Queens Jamillia, Neeyutnee, and Apailana.

Governor's boots

SLY MOORE

PALPATINE'S STAFF AIDE

SLY MOORE IS PALPATINE'S Staff Aide. She wields huge power because she controls access to the Chancellor. Moore is an Umbaran. Umbarans are known for their ability to use their minds to subtly influence, and even control, others.

Sly Moore is one of the individuals who knew of Palpatine's secret identity as Darth Sidious.

Umbarans conceal their emotions

Eyes see only in ultraviolet light

Palpatine rescued Sly Moore from a tomb haunted by long-dead Sith Lords, where a Zabrak assassin had imprisoned her. Palpatine helped her to recuperate, and their bond has been close ever since. Palpatine even trained Sly in the ways of the dark side of the Force.

Power Play

In Palpatine's administration, Sly Moore holds the post that Sei Taria had in Chancellor Valorum's time. Some whisper that Moore must have threatened the committed and dedicated Sei Taria with blackmail to persuade her to stand down.

Umbaran shadow cloak is patterned in ultraviolet colors

DATA FILE

AFFILIATION:
 Republic/Empire

HOMEWORLD: Umbara

SPECIES: Umbaran

HEIGHT: 1.78 m (5 ft 8 in)

APPEARANCES: II, III

SEE ALSO: Palpatine; Sei Taria; Chancellor Valorum

SNOWTROOPER

EXTREME-CLIMATE STORMTROOPERS

IMPERIAL SNOWTROOPERS are specialized stormtroopers that form self-sufficient mobile combat units in environments of snow and ice. Their backpacks and suit systems keep their bodies warm, while their face masks are equipped with breath heaters.

Snowtroopers carry and set up deadly E-web heavy repeating blasters in snowy terrain.

Polarized snow goggles

E-11 blaster rifle

The Empire modeled its snowtroopers on the Galactic Republic's specialized clone cold assault troopers, who fought in the Clone Wars on frozen worlds such as Orto Plutonia.

Storage pouch

Assault On Hoth

Snowtroopers are deployed as part of General Veers' Blizzard Force at the Battle of Hoth. Snowtroopers work in tandem with AT-AT walkers to effect a massive strike. They defeat the forces of the Rebel Alliance and break into Echo Base. These specialized soldiers can survive for two weeks in extreme cold terrain on suit battery power alone.

Insulated belt cape

Rugged ice boots

DATA FILE

AFFILIATION: Empire
SPECIES: Human
HEIGHT: 1.83 m (6 ft)
STANDARD EQUIPMENT:
 E-11 blaster rifle; light
 repeating blasters;
 grenades
APPEARANCES: V
SEE ALSO: Shock trooper

SPACE SLUG

GIGANTIC WORM-LIKE CREATURES

GIGANTIC EXOGORTHS, otherwise known as space slugs, survive in the airless vacuum of space. They inhabit the nooks and crannies of asteroids. Their worm-like, silicon-based bodies are typically about 10 meters (33 ft) in length, although they can grow to lengths of nearly one kilometer (0.6 mile).

Space slugs swallow silica-based mynocks, which live inside their stomachs as parasites.

Space slugs are known to inhabit the Hoth asteroid field. They are actually able to digest minerals from the asteroids on which they live. These solitary, exotic life-forms breed by splitting into two when they reach a certain size. They can then push themselves away from the surface of one asteroid and float through space to land on another.

Sensory organs

Live Prey

Han Solo unknowingly piloted the *Millennium Falcon* into the stomach of a space slug when he was escaping the Imperial fleet after the Battle of Hoth. Solo, Chewbacca, and Leia Organa could survive inside the space slug with only breath masks to provide oxygen.

Teeth for defense

DATA FILE

HOMEWORLD: Unknown

TYPICAL LENGTH:
  10 m (33 ft)

DIET: Minerals

HABITAT: Asteroids

APPEARANCES: V

SEE ALSO: Han Solo

STASS ALLIE
THOLOTHIAN JEDI MASTER

THOLOTHIAN Jedi Master Stass Allie serves the Republic during the Clone Wars. As the cousin of a highly distinguished Jedi, Adi Gallia, Allie is keen to demonstrate her own abilities. After Gallia's death in the Clone Wars, Alliee takes her place on the Jedi Council.

Stass Allie patrols Saleucami on a speeder bike, where she will lose her life to Order 66.

Common lightsaber design

Tholoth headdress

Stass Allie is a superb fighter but even more formidable is her talent for healing, which she uses to train others, including fellow Jedi Barriss Offee.

Utility belt

Tall travel boots

Brave Fighter

Stass Allie fights in Mace Windu's Jedi taskforce at the arena battle on Geonosis. She is one of the few survivors, continuing to fight as the battle escalates outside the arena. Allie and Shaak Ti later unsuccessfully attempt to protect Chancellor Palpatine from Grievous, when the General abducts him in the Battle of Coruscant.

DATA FILE

AFFILIATION: Jedi
HOMEWORLD: Tholoth
SPECIES: Tholothian
HEIGHT: 1.8 m (5 ft 9 in)
APPEARANCES: II, III
SEE ALSO: Adi Gallia; Barriss Offee

STORMTROOPER

THE EMPIRE'S ELITE SOLDIERS

STORMTROOPERS ARE THE most effective troops in the Imperial military and the most feared opponents of the Rebel Alliance. They are highly disciplined and completely loyal to the Emperor, carrying out commands without hesitation.

The massed ranks of disciplined stormtroopers obey their orders unquestioningly.

DATA FILE

AFFILIATION: Empire
SPECIES: Human
HEIGHT: 1.83 m (6 ft)
STANDARD EQUIPMENT:
E-11 blaster rifle;
thermal detonator
APPEARANCES: IV, V, VI
SEE ALSO: Snowtrooper

Blaster power cell container

Reinforced alloy plate ridge

Stormtroopers

are clones and human recruits who remain anonymous behind their white armor. This armor protects them from harsh environments and glancing shots from blaster bolts.

Fight To Win

In battle, stormtroopers are disciplined to ignore casualties within their own ranks. Notice is only taken from a tactical standpoint. Stormtroopers are never distracted by emotional responses.

Sniper position knee protector plate

Positive-grip boots

SUN FAC

POGGLE THE LESSER'S LIEUTENANT

SUN FAC IS GEONOSIAN Archduke Poggle the Lesser's chief lieutenant. His job is to ensure that Poggle's will is done throughout Geonosis. He is intelligent and skilled at playing different roles.

Clone troopers kill Sun Fac while he tries to escape after the Battle of Geonosis.

Trappings of aristocracy

DATA FILE

AFFILIATION: Separatist
HOMEWORLD: Geonosis
SPECIES: Geonosian
HEIGHT: 1.71 m (5 ft 7 in)
APPEARANCES: II
SEE ALSO: Poggle the Lesser

Exoskeletal flexibility joint

Upper-caste wings

Death Sentence

Sun Fac convicts Anakin Skywalker and Padmé Amidala of spying and sentences them to death in the Geonosian execution arena. He delivers the verdict in a courtroom packed with Separatist Senators and leaders, who look on while Skywalker and Amidala protest their innocence.

Sun Fac is an upper caste Geonosian, with wings and tusks. Like most Geonosian aristocrats, Sun Fac thinks nothing of forcing the wingless lower-caste Geonosians to work in large-scale industrial operations.

Toe structure allows Geonosians to cling to rock crags

SUPER BATTLE DROID

UPGRADED BATTLE DROID

AFTER THE TRADE FEDERATION'S defeat in the Battle of Naboo, its leaders commissioned an improved battle droid. Tougher and more heavily armed, super battle droids break Republic regulations on private security forces. However, the Neimoidians have too much influence to care.

R2-D2 has his own way of fighting super battle droids: He shoots oil at them, then sets it on fire.

The droid foundries of Geonosis secretly manufacture super battle droids. The droids have standard battle droid internal components for economy, but they utilize a much stronger shell.

Arms stronger than battle droid limbs

Monogrip hands are hard to damage

DATA FILE

AFFILIATION: Separatist

TYPE: B2 super battle droid

MANUFACTURER: Baktoid Combat Automata

HEIGHT: 1.93 m (6 ft 4 in)

APPEARANCES: II, III, CW

SEE ALSO: Battle droid

Excess heat radiated through calf vanes

Flexible armored midsection

Strap-on foot tips can be replaced with claws or pads

Fearless Droids

Super battle droids can be poor at formulating attack plans. However, they make up for this lack by their fearlessness in battle, reducing their targets to ruins.

SY SNOOTLES

LEAD VOCALIST FOR THE MAX REBO BAND

SY SNOOTLES IS A Pa'lowick singer and lead vocalist for the Max Rebo Band when they played at Jabba's palace. Snootles would only agree to join the band on the strict condition that Rebo also hired her good friend, Greeata Jendowanian, as a dancer and singer.

Pa'lowicks have round bodies, lean limbs, eye-stalks, and long lip-stalks.

Expressive mouth

Retractable tusks protrude from second mouth

Powerful chest for swimming—and singing!

In an adventurous life, Snootles has been the lover of Ziro the Hutt and, after she discovered his true cruelty, his assassin (for Jabba the Hutt). In Jabba's palace Snootles works as a double agent, feeding Bib Fortuna's lies to Jabba's enemies.

Skin coloration provides camouflage in swamps of homeworld

Strange Singing

Jabba's appreciation of Sy Snootles' singing has given her a vastly inflated idea of her own talent. When the band splits up after Jabba's death, Snootles finds it hard to make it anywhere mainstream. The chief reason being her vocals are just too weird.

Microphone stand

Forward and backward-facing toes for walking on shallow lakes

DATA FILE

AFFILIATION: Jabba's Palace
HOMEWORLD: Lowick
SPECIES: Pa'lowick
HEIGHT: 1.6 m (5 ft 3 in)
APPEARANCES: VI, CW
SEE ALSO: Max Rebo; Greeata

TARFFUL

WOOKIEE CHIEFTAIN

TARFFUL IS LEADER of the Wookiee city of Kachirho. When the Separatist forces invade his planet, Kashyyyk, Tarfful works with Chewbacca and Jedi Yoda, Luminara Unduli, and Quinlan Vos to plan the Wookiees' strategy for repelling the invaders.

Tarfful and Chewbacca help Yoda flee in a hidden escape pod after Order 66.

Teeth bared for war cry

Decorative pauldron

Orb-igniter

Long-gun

DATA FILE

AFFILIATION: Republic
HOMEWORLD: Kashyyyk
SPECIES: Wookiee
HEIGHT: 2.34 m (7 ft 8 in)
APPEARANCES: III, CW
SEE ALSO: Chewbacca

Wookiee Attack

Tarfful is a calm, considerate Wookiee who can be a mighty warrior when necessary. He leads his fellow Wookiees in daring raids on amphibious Separatist tank droids.

Tarfful was once enslaved by the Trandoshan slavers, who have long been the enemies of the Wookiees. When clone troops rescued him, Tarfful pledged to fight anyone who tried to enslave his people or capture his planet.

Thick calf muscles from climbing trees

Fur protects upper foot

TAUNTAUN

HOTH SNOW LIZARDS

TAUNTAUNS ARE SNOW LIZARDS that inhabit the ice planet Hoth. They can slow their body functions down to a standstill to survive the intensely cold nights. Tauntauns serve as mounts for the Rebel soldiers of Echo Base, who find them more reliable than their patrol vehicles in extreme winds and cold.

Han Solo uses his dead tauntaun to keep the injured Luke Skywalker warm until help arrives.

Horns for dominance combat

Tough lips for scraping lichen

Missions

Luke Skywalker and Han Solo rode tauntauns on Rebel patrol missions to position a network of life-form sensors along Echo Base's perimeter.

Tauntauns

are obedient and hardy mounts but they secrete thick oils and have an unpleasant odor. Patrol riders learn to ignore this, concentrating on the search for signs of Imperial forces.

DATA FILE

HOMEWORLD: Hoth
HEIGHT: 1.3—2 m
(4 ft 3 in—6 ft 7 in)
DIET: Omnivorous
HABITAT: Snowy plains
APPEARANCES: V
SEE ALSO: Luke Skywalker

TEEBO
EWOK MYSTIC

THE EWOK NAMED Teebo is a watcher of the stars and a poet. Teebo has a mystical connection to the forces of nature. His keen perceptive abilities and practical thinking has made Teebo a leader within his tribe.

Teebo joins the Rebel Alliance with his fellow Ewoks to defeat the Imperial army on Endor.

Authority stick

Churi feathers

Gurreck skull headdress

Teebo had many adventures growing up in his tribe, before becoming an apprentice of the tribal shaman, Logray. He is learning the ways of Ewok magic and hopes to become the Ewok shaman someday.

Hunting knife

Striped pelt

DATA FILE

AFFILIATION: Republic/ Rebel Alliance

HOMEWORLD: Endor

SPECIES: Ewok

HEIGHT: 1 m (3 ft 3 in)

APPEARANCES: VI

SEE ALSO: Logray

Aggressive Beginnings

When Teebo first sees Han Solo and his team, he distrusts them. After being freed from his bonds, R2-D2 promptly zaps Teebo's backside!

TEN NUMB

B-WING PILOT

SULLUSTAN PILOT TEN NUMB flies a B-wing starfighter at the Battle of Endor. His Blue Squadron heroically pummels Darth Vader's flagship, the *Executor,* with laser blasts, drawing Imperial fire away from the rest of the Rebel strike force.

At the Battle of Endor, Ten Numb piloted the B-wing code-named Blue Five.

Insulated helmet

Flak vest

DATA FILE

AFFILIATION: Rebel Alliance
HOMEWORLD: Sullust
SPECIES: Sullustan
HEIGHT: 1.5 m (4 ft 11 in)
APPEARANCES: VI
SEE ALSO: Luke Skywalker

Chest pack straps

Dedicated Pilot

B-wing starfighters are some of the largest and most heavily armed ships in the Rebel Alliance fleet. The main wing of the ship can rotate around the fixed cockpit, so that the pilot always stays upright. After the Battle of Endor, Ten Numb is promoted to Blue Leader. He helps extinguish the fires on Endor's forest moon caused by falling debris in the space battle. To do this, he flies a B-wing retrofitted with sprayers.

Sullustans

Sullustans are humanoids from the Outer Rim planet Sullust. They have large black eyes, facial jowls named dewflaps, and large ears. Before Ten Numb joined the Alliance, he was a bounty hunter and demolitions expert.

Gear harness

TESSEK
JABBA'S QUARREN ACCOUNTANT

TESSEK IS EMPLOYED at Jabba's palace as the Hutt's accountant. But his loyalty to Jabba is a smokescreen. Behind the crime lord's back, Tessek plots to assassinate him and take over his criminal empire. But Tessek is too clever not to know that Jabba probably knows this, too.

The Quarren are one of several aquatic species from the planet Mon Calamari.

Suction-tipped fingers

Hearing organs

Manipulative mouth tentacles

DATA FILE

AFFILIATION: Jabba's entourage
HOMEWORLD: Mon Calamari
SPECIES: Quarren
HEIGHT: 1.8 m (5 ft 11in)
APPEARANCES: VI
SEE ALSO: Jabba the Hutt

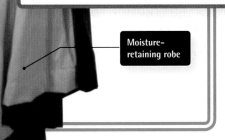

Tessek is a Quarren from Mon Calamari. He was involved in galactic politics until the Empire began to enslave his people. This caused Tessek to go into hiding on Tatooine, where he found use for his financial skills among the Hutt gangsters.

Best Laid Plans

Tessek plans to detonate a bomb on board Jabba's sail barge. So the calculating Quarren is extremely anxious when Jabba insists he join the party to the Sarlacc pit at Carkoon. Tessek escapes on a speeder bike after the battle, but is unable to escape the B'omarr monks, who decide his brain should be removed from his body.

Moisture-retaining robe

TIE FIGHTER PILOT

IMPERIAL PILOTS

TIE FIGHTER PILOTS form an elite group within the Imperial navy. These black-suited pilots are conditioned to be entirely dedicated to the mission and to destroying their targets, even if this causes their own deaths.

TIE targeting systems and flight controls are superior to anything available to Rebel fighters.

Reinforced flight helmet

Gas transfer hose

Life support pack

Fighter pilots take great pride in their TIE fighters, even though the ships lack deflector shields, hyperdrives, ejection equipment, or life support systems. TIE pilots view all these things as tools of cowards.

Vacuum g-suit

Energy-shielded fabric

Uniform

The Empire keeps TIE fighter pilots on a constant state of alert so they are ready for battle at any time. TIE fighter pilots wear reinforced flight helmets, with breather tubes connected to a life support pack. Pilots rely on their self-contained flight suits to stay alive in their ships when they are in space.

DATA FILE

AFFILIATION: Empire
SPECIES: Human
STANDARD VEHICLE:
TIE-series starfighters
APPEARANCES: IV, V, VI
SEE ALSO: AT-AT pilot

TION MEDON

PORT ADMINISTRATOR OF PAU CITY

TION MEDON IS MASTER of port Administration for Pau City on Utapau. Now MagnaGuards have killed his committee members and the Separatist leadership is using his world as a temporary sanctuary.

Utapau's surface is windswept and barren. Its people live in cities within huge sinkholes.

DATA FILE

AFFILIATION: Republic
HOMEWORLD: Utapau
SPECIES: Pau'an
HEIGHT: 2.06 m (6 ft 7 in)
APPEARANCES: III
SEE ALSO: Pau'an Warrior

Wide belt supports bony frame

Gray, furrowed skin from lack of light in sinkholes

Port master's walking stick

Tion Medon is a descendent of Timon Medon, who unified Utapau. Like all Pau'ans, Tion prefers darkness to sunlight and raw meat to cooked.

Reassurance

When Jedi Obi-Wan Kenobi lands at Pau City on Utapau, Tion Medon reassures the Jedi that nothing strange has happened. While Kenobi's ship is refueled, Tion whispers that Separatists have taken control of Utapau.

Floor-length robes are a recent fashion

TUSKEN RAIDER
FIERCE TATOOINE NOMADS

TUSKEN RAIDERS, OR SAND PEOPLE, are fierce nomads on Tatooine. They compete with human settlers for precious moisture on the desert planet, prowling remote areas, surviving where no others can. Tusken Raiders capture Anakin Skywalker's mother, Shmi, and drag her to their encampment.

Anakin Skywalker releases his vengeful fury on the Tusken encampment.

Silent Attacker

Sand People are often taller than humans, yet they blend into the landscape with unsettling ease. They sometimes scavenge or steal from the edges of settlement zones. Only the sound of the feared Krayt dragon is enough to scare the Sand People away.

Gaderffii stick made from scavenged metal

Eye-protection lenses

Moisture trap

Thick desert cloak

Sand People wear heavy clothing to protect them from the planet's harsh suns. They keep their faces hidden behind head bandages. Their traditional weapon is an ax, named a gaderffii (or "gaffi") stick.

DATA FILE

AFFILIATION: Non-affiliated
HOMEWORLD: Tatooine
SPECIES: Tusken
HEIGHT: 1.8 m (5 ft 11 in)
APPEARANCES: I, II, IV
SEE ALSO: Bantha

UGNAUGHT
PORCINE SPECIES ON CLOUD CITY

UGNAUGHTS WERE SOLD INTO slavery long ago from their home planet Gentes. The eccentric explorer Lord Ecclessis Figg brought in three Ugnaught tribes to help build Cloud City on Bespin. In return, he gave them the freedom of the city.

Ugnaughts perform the often dangerous work of mining and processing tibanna gas.

Tusks used in blood duels

Captain's stripes

At least one Ugnaught has begun a new life away from Bespin. Yoxgit made a fortune illegally selling tibanna gas to arms dealers, then jumped planet for Tatooine, where he finds work with Jabba the Hutt.

Flight gauntlets

Stocky body is efficient at working for long periods

Expensive tactical boots

Cloud City Workers

Ugnaught workers in the depths of Cloud City sort through discarded metal junk, where C-3PO nearly ends up after he is blasted to pieces. The species has constructed a network of humid, red-lighted work corridors and tunnels throughout the city, most of which can only be navigated by their species.

DATA FILE

AFFILIATION: Non-affiliated
HOMEWORLD: Gentes
SPECIES: Ugnaught
APPROX. HEIGHT: 1 m (3 ft 3 in)
APPEARANCES: V, VI, CW
SEE ALSO: Jabba the Hutt

UTAI
WORKERS ON UTAPAU

THE HUMBLE AND STOCKY Utai are workers in the sinkholes and caverns of their homeworld, Utapau. They are animal handlers and workers in the various landing platforms. The Utai's distended eyes give them keen night vision for seeing in the darkness of rock caverns.

Utai mechanics attend to Obi-Wan Kenobi's ship when he lands in Pau City on Utapau.

Long ago, only the Utai lived in Utapau's sinkholes, until climate change forced the lordly Pau'ans from the planet surface. Now the two species work in harmony together to form a peaceful society.

Eyes on stalks

Stubby four-fingered hand

Varactyl muck boots

Ancient Skills

The Utai's traditional homes are in the crevices of the planet's sinkholes. Long ago, the Utai learned how to domesticate the carnivorous, flying dactillions by feeding them with fresh meat. They also tamed the varactyl lizards that are used as transport on Utapau, and still serve as wranglers for the dragon mounts.

DATA FILE

AFFILIATION: Republic
HOMEWORLD: Utapau
SPECIES: Utai
HEIGHT: 1.22 m (4 ft)
APPEARANCES: III
SEE ALSO: Tion Medon

WAMPA
RAVENOUS ICE CREATURES

HUGE WAMPA ICE CREATURES hunt tauntauns and other creatures on the snow plains of Hoth, where their howling wails blend with the icy winds at night. They are normally solitary beasts but have been known to band together to make raids on human settlements. Wampas often attack the Rebel base on Hoth.

Luke Skywalker returns to consciousness hanging upside down in a wampa cave.

Curving horns

Fanged mouth

Camouflaging white pelt

Tautaun bone

DATA FILE

HOMEWORLD: Hoth
HEIGHT: 3 m (9 ft 10 in)
DIET: Carnivorous
HABITAT: Snow plains
APPEARANCES: V
SEE ALSO: Tauntaun

Thick insulating fur

Wampas' shaggy
white fur provides warmth and camouflage in the snowy conditions of Hoth. These cunning predators stalk their prey before lunging at it, using their powerful arms to stun it.

Hungry Beast
Wampas sate their hunger on freshly killed tauntaun meat. Human flesh is relatively unknown to wampas, but highly prized.

WAT TAMBOR

FOREMAN OF THE TECHNO UNION

WAT TAMBOR IS FOREMAN of the Techno Union, a powerful commercial body that makes massive profits from new technologies. He is also an Executive of arms manufacturer, Baktoid Armor Workshop.

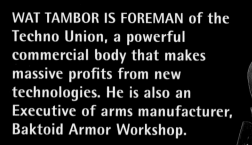

Darth Vader shows no mercy to Wat Tambor on Mustfatar.

Vocabulator/annunciator

DATA FILE

AFFILIATION: Separatist
HOMEWORLD: Skako
SPECIES: Skakoan
HEIGHT: 1.93 m (6 ft 4 in)
APPEARANCES: II, III, CW
SEE ALSO: Darth Vader; Boba Fett

Dials control vocabulator

Close Calls

Wat Tambor has suffered several close calls during the Clone Wars. The Republic took him captive on Metalorn and he narrowly escaped an assassination attempt by Boba Fett on Xagobah. With his homeworld Skako in Republic hands, Tambor has no option but to place his trust in the Separatist leaders.

Tambor left his home planet Skako at an early age and began a career in technology on the harsh industrial world of Metalorn. Few Skakoans leave their world due to its unique atmospheric pressure. In fact, Tambor must wear a special suit to avoid his body exploding in standard, oxygen-based atmospheres.

Rich outer tunic over exo-suit

WATTO

TOYDARIAN JUNK DEALER

WATTO IS A SHARP-WITTED, flying Toydarian shopkeeper who owns a spare parts business in Mos Eisley on Tatooine. He has a sharp eye for a bargain and spends his proceeds at Podraces, gambling with Hutts, and winning slaves— including Anakin and Shmi Skywalker.

Watto insists his shop is a parts dealership, though most call it a junk shop.

Flexible trunk-like nose

Three-day stubble

Pudgy belly mostly composed of gas

Keycodes for main safe and slave keepers

Chance Meeting

When Watto meets an off-worlder looking for spare hyperdrive parts, he sees an opportunity for some profitable swindling. Jedi Qui-Gon Jinn does not suspect that he will meet the prophesied Chosen One, Anakin Skywalker, in this very shop. Losing Anakin to the Jedi is the start of a downward spiral for Watto, who eventually loses his other slave, Shmi, too.

Watto was a soldier on his homeworld Toydaria, but left the planet after suffering an injury. On Tatooine, he watched how the Jawas sold used goods, learning some of their tricks, before setting up his own business.

DATA FILE

AFFILIATION: Republic
HOMEWORLD: Toydaria
SPECIES: Toydarian
HEIGHT: 1.37 m (4 ft 6 in)
APPEARANCES: I, II
SEE ALSO: Qui-Gon Jinn; Anakin Skywalker; Shmi Skywalker

WICKET W. WARRICK

YOUNG EWOK LONER

Wicket W. Warrick is a young Ewok with a reputation as a loner. He spends much time wandering far from his village in the forests of Endor's moon. Wicket is on one of his travels when he runs into Princess Leia Organa. He helps her to the safety of his treetop village, and soon comes to trust her.

Wicket's knowledge of the forest assists the Rebels in their attack on the Imperial forces.

DATA FILE

AFFILIATION: Republic
HOMEWORLD: Endor
SPECIES: Ewok
HEIGHT: .8 m (2 ft 7 in)
APPEARANCES: VI
SEE ALSO: Princess Leia; Teebo; Logray; Chief Chirpa

Young

Wicket had an adventurous childhood with his great friend Teebo. Wicket became a pupil of the medicine man Logray, but he lacked patience and spoke out against Logray's dark magic rituals. Logray turned against Wicket, and made him feel unwelcome in the village.

Friends?

Having befriended Leia, when her friends arrive, Wicket argues that they should be spared any abuse. But his solitary habits leave him with a big lack of influence among the elders in his Bright Tree village.

Hood

Thick fur

Spear

X-WING PILOTS

REBEL ALLIANCE PILOTS

MANY X-WING pilots of Red Squadron become legendary figures in the Rebel Alliance. Pilots such as Biggs Darklighter ("Red Three"), Wedge Antilles ("Red Two"), and Luke Skywalker ("Red Five") are crucial to the destruction of the first Death Star.

Luke's childhood friend Biggs Darklighter takes part in the assault on the first Death Star.

Life support unit

Insulated helmet

Alliance symbol

Red Squadron fly
T-65 X-wing starfighters. These ships are equipped with droid sockets for astromech droids, long-range laser cannons, and a small payload of proton torpedoes.

Wedge Antilles

A native of Corellia, Wedge Antilles is one of just two X-wing pilots, with Luke Skywalker, who survive the Battle of Yavin, in which the Empire's Death Star is destroyed. Antilles flies a snowspeeder at the Battle of Hoth, and is the leader of Red Squadron at the Battle of Endor.

Equipment pocket

Gear harness

Signal flares

DATA FILE

AFFILIATION: Rebel Alliance
SPECIES: Human
STANDARD VEHICLE: X-wing starfighter
APPEARANCES: IV
SEE ALSO: Luke Skywalker

YADDLE
JEDI MASTER

SITTING ON THE JEDI HIGH COUNCIL, Master Yaddle offers few words but much compassion and balanced patience. She looks up to Master Yoda, being the same species as him, but is about half his age (Yaddle is only 477!). Yaddle has trained many Jedi Padawans, including fellow Council member Oppo Rancisis.

Yaddle must help to judge whether Qui-Gon Jinn's instincts about Anakin are correct.

DATA FILE

AFFILIATION: Jedi
HOMEWORLD: Unknown
SPECIES: Unknown
HEIGHT: 61 cm (2 ft)
APPEARANCES: I
SEE ALSO: Yoda; Oppo Rancisis

Yaddle is one of the few Jedi permitted to practice morichro. This ancient art enables the user to rapidly slow down an opponent's bodily functions to the point of death.

Youthful topknot

Shapely ears

Mind and Body

Yaddle has devoted a lot of time to scholarly interests, and spends much time in the Jedi archives. But she has been an active Jedi in the field, too. Yaddle's final mission is with Obi-Wan Kenobi and Anakin Skywalker, when she sacrifices her life to save the people of Mawan by using the Force to absorb a deadly biological weapon.

YARAEL POOF

QUERMIAN JEDI MASTER

JEDI MASTER YARAEL POOF is a member of the High Council at the time of the Naboo crisis and the start of the Clone Wars. He is a master of specialized Jedi mind tricks, which he can use to bring conflicts to a decisive end.

Poof has a mischievous side and enjoys playing mind tricks on colleagues.

Extended neck

DATA FILE

AFFILIATION: Jedi
HOMEWORLD: Quermia
SPECIES: Quermian
HEIGHT: 2.64 m (8 ft 8 in)
APPEARANCES: I
SEE ALSO: Obi-Wan Kenobi; Qui-Gon Jinn

Traditional Quermian cannom collar

Selfless Jedi

Yarael Poof is a dexterous combatant with a lightsaber, perfecting many incredible moves that only his spineless anatomy can allow. However, Yarael loses his life defending the billions of inhabitants of Coruscant from an ancient artifact being wielded by a dangerous revolutionary.

Robe hides second pair of arms and chest with lower brain

Quermians have extended necks and long limbs, as well as a second pair of arms, which Poof hides under his Jedi robe. The species is noseless, as they smell with olfactory glands in their hands. Quermians also have two brains—an upper brain in the head and a lower brain in the chest.

YARNA
ASKAJIAN DANCER AT JABBA'S PALACE

YARNA D'AL GARGAN has been a dancer at Jabba's palace for many years. The daughter of an Askajian tribal chief, Yarna was captured by slavers and transported to Tatooine, where Jabba bought her. Jabba's cruel whim is to force Yarna to wear special makeup to make her look more like his mother.

Yarna performs highly exotic dances for Jabba's pleasure.

Body enlarged to resemble a Hutt

Makeup hides Yarna's true beauty

On Askaji, Yarna had
been married with four cublings. She danced only for the honor of her tribe. After Jabba bought her and her family, the Hutt fed her husband, Nautag, to his rancor for insubordination and kept the cublings in his Mos Eisley townhouse.

Better Future
Yarna hates Jabba, but has become close to some of the palace regulars. After the Hutt's death, Yarna escapes his hated palace and is reunited with her precious cublings. She will later dance at the wedding of Han Solo and Leia Organa!

Tribal skirt

DATA FILE

AFFILIATION: Jabba's entourage
HOMEWORLD: Askaji
SPECIES: Askajian
HEIGHT: 1.5 m (5 ft 11 in)
APPEARANCES: VI
SEE ALSO: Jabba the Hutt

YODA

LEGENDARY JEDI MASTER

YODA IS ONE OF THE most powerful Jedi ever and has lived to be nearly 900 years old. He served the Galactic Republic at its height, as well as through its decline and fall. Yoda is one of the few Jedi to survive the Clone Wars—he goes into hiding on the remote planet Dagobah.

On Dagobah, Yoda trains Luke Skywalker, his final student and the galaxy's last hope.

Pensive expression

Head has been nearly bald for centuries

Homespun robe

DATA FILE

AFFILIATION: Jedi
HOMEWORLD: Unknown
SPECIES: Unknown
HEIGHT: 66 cm (2 ft 2 in)
APPEARANCES: I, II, III, V, VI, CW
SEE ALSO: Luke Skywalker

Yoda has guided hundreds of Jedi to knighthood and visited countless worlds. Yoda takes quiet satisfaction in his ability to resolve conflict by nonviolent means, until the re-emergence of the dark side unseats even others' confidence in him.

Sith Fury

Accepting finally that the Clone Wars have been nothing more than a manipulation by the Sith to destroy the Jedi Order, Yoda confronts Palpatine. Even the diminutive Jedi's amazing strength and speed, however, is not a match for the devastating fury of a Sith Lord.

YUZZUM
MUSICAL ALIENS FROM ENDOR

YUZZUM ARE FURRY ALIENS with long, spindly limbs. They share their homeworld, the forest moon of Endor, with the Ewoks. Yuzzum speak a musical-sounding language that makes them natural singers. Jabba's palace is home to two Yuzzum: singer Joh Yowsa and sharp-shooter Wam Lufba (nicknamed "Blam"!).

Wam Lufba keeps an eye on strange new arrivals at Jabba's palace.

Nasal organs can smell sounds

Matted fur

Singer
Joh Yowza sings in the Max Rebo Band at Jabba's palace. Yowza was a runt on Endor and excluded from others' activities, so he kept to himself and began to sing. He got a passage off-world on a spacer's ship and started singing in bands. After Jabba's death, he forms a new band with Rystáll Sant and Greeata Jendowanian.

Blaster rifle

Wam Lufba is a Yuzzum vermin exterminator who ends up in Jabba's palace. Lufba came to Jabba's attention when he blasted his way out of his rancor pit. Impressed, Jabba made him one of his henchmen. He and Joh Yowza have become friends.

Forest boots

202

ZAM WESELL

SHAPE-CHANGING ASSASSIN

ZAM WESELL is a hired assassin with a special edge. As a Clawdite shape-shifter, Wesell can change her appearance to mimic the appearance of other species. For some years, Zam has worked with renowned bounty hunter Jango Fett.

In her true Clawdite form, Zam Wesell is a reptilian humanoid.

Zam Wesell was born on Zolan, the home of the Mabari, an ancient order of warrior-knights. The Mabari trained Zam until her desire for wealth took her to the vast metropolis of Denon, where she employed her skills and training as an assassin.

Bodysuit stretches to allow shape-shifting

Direct-to-lungs breathpack

KYD-21 blaster

Blast-energy skirt

DATA FILE

AFFILIATION: Bounty hunter
HOMEWORLD: Zolan
SPECIES: Clawdite
HEIGHT: 1.68 m (5 ft 6 in)
APPEARANCES: II
SEE ALSO: Jango Fett

Airspeeder Chase

Zam Wesell often steals a new vehicle for each job, to avoid being traced. But Wesell uses her own airspeeder when she knows she needs to get away fast. When Zam takes on a job for Jango Fett—to kill Senator Padmé Amidala—she has to outrun two Jedi Knights in a borrowed speeder who are hard on her trail.

Boots accept a variety of limb forms

ZETT JUKASSA
JEDI PADAWAN

ZETT JUKASSA IS THE JEDI Padawan of Jedi Knight Mierme Unill. Zett shows great talent with a lightsaber, but does not neglect his mind either, making use of the extensive Jedi Archives in the Jedi Temple on Coruscant.

Zett puts up a brave defense during the devastating raid on the Jedi Temple.

Short hair of a Padawan apprentice

Apprentice's long braid

Zett's parents sent him to the Jedi Temple as a baby, as soon as they spotted his strong Force potential. Zett has gifts of farsight, and receives visions of his parents and homeworld, though he knew neither.

Utility belt

Jedi tunic has only been worn for training

Shot Down

Zett is in the Jedi Temple when Darth Vader and a detachment of clone troopers arrive to carry out a massacre. Zett fights nobly, striking down many clone troopers. He nearly reaches a speeder owned by Bail Organa, but Clone Sergeant Fox blasts him before he can reach the Senator.

Training boots

DATA FILE

AFFILIATION: Jedi
HOMEWORLD: Mon Gazza
SPECIES: Human
HEIGHT: 1.57 m (5 ft 2 in)
APPEARANCES: II, III
SEE ALSO: Bail Organa;
   Clone trooper (Phase II)

ZUCKUSS

GAND BOUNTY HUNTER

ZUCKUSS IS AN INSECTOID Gand bounty hunter who often partners with droid bounty hunter 4-LOM. Zuckuss is a tireless tracker, who uses Force abilities and the mystic findsman traditions that date back centuries on his fog-swept home planet, Gand.

Zuckuss is renowned for his tracking skills and is a highly sought-after bounty hunter.

DATA FILE

AFFILIATION: Bounty hunter
HOMEWORLD: Gand
SPECIES: Gand
HEIGHT: 1.5 m (4 ft 11 in)
APPEARANCES: V
SEE ALSO: 4-LOM

Compound eyes

Ammonia respirator

Findsman body cloak

Heavy battle armor under cloak

Breather packs

Zuckuss breathes only ammonia so wears a respirator in oxygen-based atmospheres. When his planet's findsman traditions began dying out, Zuckuss became one of the first findsmen to go off-world. Bounty hunting is now a lucrative way for him to use his particular talents.

Powerful Pair

Zuckuss's uncanny abilities make other bounty hunters uneasy. But not 4-LOM, whom Zuckuss partners with many times. The two bounty hunters make a formidable team. The pairing does not go unnoticed by Darth Vader, who hires them to locate the *Falcon* by infiltrating the Rebel Alliance.

INDEX

2-1B **4**
4-LOM **5**, 205
8D8 **6**

A
Ackbar, Admiral **10**, 77
acklay **8**
Allie, Stass 9, 54, **178**
Amedda, Mas 39, **115**
Amidala, Padmé 14, 17 29, 34, 37, 38, 39, 41, 57, 81, 99, 122, 123, 125, 132, **133**, 141, 146, 148, 158, 169, 170, 174, 180, 203
Antilles, Captain 35
Antilles, Wedge 197
Apailana, Queen **146**
Arana, Koffi 32
Argente, Passel **135**
astromech droids 6, 33, 61, 69, 74, 91, 108, 148, 149, 150, 151, 185
AT-AT pilot **15**
AT-ST pilot **16**
A-wing pilot **18**

B
Baba, Ponda 63, **143**
Bacara, Commander 50, 102
bantha **21**
Battle droid **24**, 66, 87, 127, 129, 168, 181
Bibble, Sio **174**
Billaba, Depa 60
Binks, Jar Jar 49, **99**, 130, 138, 163
Bly, Commander **51**
Boga **28**
B'omarr monk **19**, 95, 187
Bossk **30**
bounty hunters
    4-LOM **5**
    Bossk **30**
    Boushh **31**
    Fett, Boba **27**
    Fett, Jango **98**
    Greedo **84**
    IG-88 **89**
    Sing, Aurra **17**
    Wessel, Zam **203**
    Zuckuss 5, **205**
Bouri, Omo 160
Boushh **31**
Buzz droid **33**

C
C-3PO 6, **34**, 40, 42, 61, 69, 74, 107, 108, 144, 161
Calrissian, Lando 75, **106**, 107, 124, 157
Chewbacca 16, 31, **40**, 86, 107, 108, 177, 183
Chalmun 71
Chirpa, Chief **42**, 108

clone commanders
    Bacara **50**
    Bly **51**
    Cody **52**
    Gree **53**
    Neyo **54**
clone pilot **45**
clone trooper (Phase I) **46**, 47
clone trooper (Phase II) **47**
Cody, Commander **52**, 127
colo claw fish **49**
Cordé 38
Crab droid **56**
Cracken, General **75**
creatures
    acklay **8**
    bantha **21**
    Boga **28**
    colo claw fish **49**
    dactillion 136, 192
    dewback **61**
    opee sea killer **130**
    rancor **152**
    reek **155**
    sando aqua monster **163**
    sarlacc **165**
    space slug **177**
    tauntaun **184**
    varactyl 28, 192
    wampa **193**
Crumb, Salacious **161**
Crynyd, Arvel 18

D
dactillion 136, 192
D'an, Figrin **71**
Darklighter, Biggs 197
Death Star gunner **59**
dewback **61**
Dodonna, Jan **97**
Dooku, Count 48, **55**, 76, 80, 101, 110, 113, 137, 141, 162, 173
Drallig, Cin **43**
Droideka **64**
droids
    2-1B **4**
    4-LOM **5**, 205
    8D8 **6**
    astromech see astromech droids
    battle **24**
    buzz **33**
    C-3PO **34**
    crab **56**
    droideka **64**
    dwarf spider **66**
    EV-9D9 **69**
    FX-series med **72**
    GH-7 medical **81**
    GNK ("gonk") **144**
    hailfire **85**
    homing spider **87**
    IG-88 **89**
    interrogator **94**
    MagnaGuard **113**

medical 4, 72, 81
    MSE ("mouse") 91
    octuptarra **127**
    OOM-9 **129**
    pilot **137**
    pit **138**
    power 6, **144**
    probot **92**
    protocol see protocol droids
    R2-D2 **148**
    R2-Q5 91
    R4-G9 **149**
    R4-P17 **150**
    R5-D4 **151**
    RA-7 91
    security **168**
    super battle **181**
Dwarf spider droid **66**

E
EV-9D9 **69**
Evazan, Doctor **63**
Ewoks
    Chirpa, Chief **42**
    Logray **108**
    Teebo **185**
    Warrick, Wicket W. **196**

F
Fac, Sun **180**
Fett, Boba 17, **27**, 30, 89, 157, 165, 194
Fett, Jango 46, 48, 51, **98**, 203
Figg, Lord Ecclessis **191**
Fisto, Kit 7, **103**
Fortuna, Bib **26**, 128, 152, 161
FX-series med droid **72**

G
Gallia, Adi **9**, 160, 178
Gamorrean guard **73**, 152
Garindan **74**
Gasgano **140**
Geonosian soldier **80**
GH-7 medical droid **81**
Giiett, Micah 32
Greeata **83**, 157, 182, 202
Gree, Commander **53**
Greedo **84**
Grievous, General 28, **76**, 127, 136, 149, 162, 168
Gunray, Nute **125**, 156, 173, 174

H
Haako, Rune **156**
Hailfire droid **85**
handmaidens 38, 158
Hill, San **162**, 173
Homing spider droid **87**
Hoth Rebel trooper **88**
Hutt, Zorba the **96**

I
IG-88 **89**
Imperial dignitary **90**
Imperial droids **91**
Imperial officers
    Jerjerrod, Moff **117**
    Needa, Captain **36**
    Ozzel, Admiral **11**
    Piett, Admiral **12**
    Tarkin, Grand Moff **82**
    Veers, General **79**
Imperial probot **92**
Imperial Red Guard **93**
Interrogator droid **94**

J
Jabba the Hutt 5, 6, 19, 30, 31, 65, 69, 71, 73, 83, 95, **96**, 106, 109, 114, 116, 119, 128, 152, 157, 159, 165, 182, 187, 191, 200, 202
Jamillia, Queen 37
Jawa **100**, 132
Jedi
    Allie, Stass **178**
    Arana, Koffi 32
    Billaba, Depa 60
    Bouri, Omo 160
    Drallig, Cin **43**
    Fisto, Kit 7, **103**
    Gallia, Adi **9**
    Giiett, Micah 32
    Jinn, Qui-Gon **147**
    Jukassa, Zett 204
    Kenobi, Obi-Wan **126**
    Ki-Adi-Mundi **102**
    Kolar, Agen **13**
    Koon, Plo **139**
    Koth, Eeth **67**
    Nu, Jocasta **101**
    Offee, Barriss **23**
    Piell, Even **70**
    Poof, Yarael **199**
    Rancisis, Oppo **131**
    Secura, Aayla **7**
    Skywalker, Anakin **14**
    Skywalker, Luke **109**
    Swan, Bultar 32
    Tano, Ahsoka 139, 170
    Ti, Shaak **170**
    Tiin, Saesee **160**
    Trebor, Coleman **48**
    Unduli, Luminara **110**
    Vos, Quinlan 7, **183**
    Windu, Mace **112**
    Yaddle **198**
    Yoda **201**
Jerjerrod, Moff 93, **117**
Jettster, Dexter **62**
Jinn, Qui-Gon 49, 57, 67, 70, 99, 126, 130, **147**, 163, 168, 195, 198
J'Quille 95
Jukassa, Zett **204**

K

Kabe 119
Kee, Denaria 135
Kee, Neva 140
Kenobi, Obi-Wan 8, 14, 20, 25,
    28, 33, 43, 49, 52, 57, 58,
    62, 63, 68, 74, 76, 98, 101,
    113, 119, 120, 123, **126**,
    130, 136, 141, 147, 148,
    149, 163, 168, 170, 189,
    198
Ki-Adi-Mundi 50, **102**
Kolar, Agen 13
Koon, Plo 32, 67, **139**
Koth, Eeth 13, **67**
Kylantha, Queen 146

L

Lars, Aika 44, 132
Lars, Beru **25**, 132
Lars, Cliegg **44**, 132, 171
Lars, Owen 25, 44, **132**
Leia, Princess 20, 31, 35, 61,
    78, 82, 86, 94, 95, 96, 107,
    126, **145**, 148, 177, 196
Lobot **107**
Lograp **108**, 185, 196
Lufba, Wam 202

M

Madine, General 75, **77**
MagnaGuard **113**, 189
Mai, Shu 51, **173**
Malakili **114**
Mandrell, Ody 138
Maul, Darth **57**, 147
Mawhonic 140
McCool, Droopy **65**
Me, Lyn 83, **111**
Medon, Tion **189**
Modal Nodes 71
Moore, Sly 169, **175**
Mothma, Mon **118**
Muftak **119**
Mustafarian (Northern) **120**
Mustafarian (Southern) **121**

N

Naboo Guard **122**
Naboo monarchs 37, 133,
    146, 174
Nass, Boss **29**
Needa, Captain **36**
Neeyutnee, Queen 174
nexu **123**
Neyo, Commander **54**
Nu, Jocasta **101**
Numb, Ten **186**
Nunb, Nien 75, **124**

O

Octuptarra droid **127**
Offee, Barriss **23**
Oola **128**
OOM-9 **129**
opee sea killer **130**
Organa, Bail **20**, 34, 35, 118
Organa, Breha 20
Ozzel, Admiral **11**, 12

P

Palpatine 20, 22, 36, 39, 41,
    52, 58, 76, 82, 90, 93, 99,
    103, 104, 112, 115, 118,
    134, 135, 160, 168, 169,
    172, 175, 178, 179, 201
Panaka, Captain **37**, 38, 122,
    174
Papanoida, Baron **22**, 41, 84
Papanoida, Che Amanwe 22, 84
Papanoida, Chi Eekway 22, **41**,
    84
Papanoida, Ion 22
Pau'ans 136, 189, 192
Pau'an warrior **136**
Piell, Even **70**
Piett, Admiral 11, **12**
Pilot droid **137**
Pit droid **138**
Podracers 138, **140**, 167
Poggle the Lesser **141**, 180
Polis Massan **142**
Poof, Yarael **199**
Power droid 6, **144**
protocol droids 5, 6, 34, 40,
    42, 61, 69, 74, 91, 107, 108,
    144, 161

R

R2-D2 6, 33, 34, 61, 74, 108,
    148, 185
R2-Q5 91
R4-G9 **149**
R4-P17 33, 149, **150**
R5-D4 **151**
RA-7 91
Rancisis, Oppo **131**, 198
rancor 114, 128, **152**, 202
Rappertunie **153**
Rebel Alliance
    Ackbar, Admiral **10**
    Antilles, Captain **35**
    Antilles, Wedge 197
    A-wing pilot **18**
    Calrissian, Lando **106**
    Chewbacca **40**
    Chirpa, Chief **42**
    Cracken, General **75**
    Darklighter, Biggs 197
    Dodonna, Jan **97**
    Hoth rebel trooper **88**
    Leia, Princess **145**
    Logray **108**
    Madine, General **77**
    Mothma, Mon **118**
    Numb, Ten **186**
    Nunb, Nien **124**
    Organa, Bail **20**
    Rebel trooper **154**
    Rieekan, General **78**
    Skywalker, Luke **109**
    Solo, Han **86**
    Teebo **185**
    X-wing pilots **197**
Rebel trooper 88, **154**
Rebo, Max 83, 111, **116**, 153,
    157, 202
reek **155**
Rieekan, General **78**
Rystáll 83, **157**, 202

S

Sabé **158**
Saelt-Marae **159**
Sai, Ko **104**
sando aqua monster **163**
Sand Person see Tusken Raider
Sandtrooper 61, **164**
sarlacc 159, **165**
Scout trooper **166**
Sebulba **167**
Secura, Aayla **7**, 51, 149
Security droid **168**
Separatists
    Argente, Passel **135**
    Battle droid **24**
    Buzz droid **33**
    Crab droid **56**
    Dooku, Count **55**
    Droideka **64**
    Dwarf spider droid **66**
    Fac, Sun **180**
    Geonosian soldier **80**
    Grievous, General **76**
    Gunray, Nute **125**
    Haako, Rune **156**
    Hailfire droid **85**
    Hill, San **162**
    Homing spider droid **87**
    MagnaGuard **113**
    Mai, Shu **173**
    Octuptarra droid **127**
    OOM-9 **129**
    Poggle the Lesser **141**
    Security droid **168**
    Tambor, Wat **194**
shock trooper **172**
Sidious, Darth 52, 103, 125,
    134, 135, 141, 156, 160,
    175 see also Palpatine
Sifo-Dyas 105
Sing, Aurra **17**, 30
Sith
    Maul, Darth **57**
    Sidious, Darth 52, 103, 125,
        134, 135, 141, 156, 160,
        175
    Starkiller 170
    Tyranus, Darth 55, 76
    Vader, Darth **58**
Skywalker, Anakin **14**, 17,
    25, 34, 43, 44, 67, 70, 84,
    112, 113, 120, 123, 126,
    129, 132, 133, 141, 147,
    170, 171, 180, 190, 195,
    198
Skywalker, Luke 4, 25, 34, 58,
    63, 72, 74, 108, **109**, 114,
    116, 119, 126, 128, 132,
    148, 152, 165, 184, 197
Skywalker, Shmi 34, 44, **171**,
    190, 195
Sleazebaggano, Elan **68**
Snit see McCool, Droopy
Snootles, Sy 83, **182**
Snowtrooper 79, **176**
Solo, Han 31, 40, 74, 77,
    84, **86**, 106, 107, 108,
    109, 116, 177, 184
space slug **177**
Stormtrooper 25, **179**
Su, Lama **105**
Super battle droid **181**
Swan, Bultar **32**

T

Tambor, Wat **194**
Tano, Ahsoka 139, 170
Tarfful 40, **183**
Taria, Sei **169**, 175
Tarkin, Grand Moff 10, **82**
tauntaun **184**
Teebo **185**
Tessek **187**
TIE fighter pilot **188**
Ti, Shaak **170**, 178
Tiin, Saesee **160**
torture droid see Interrogator
    droid
Trebor, Coleman **48**
Tusken Raider 21, 44, 114, 171,
    190
Typho, Captain **38**
Tyranus, Darth 76
    see also Dooku, Count

U

Ugnaught **191**
Unduli, Luminara 23, **110**,
    183
Utai **192**

V

Vader, Darth 4, 5, 11, 12, 18,
    30, 32, 34, 35, 36, 43, **58**,
    72, 79, 92, 93, 94, 106,
    107, 109, 117, 126, 132,
    156, 170, 172, 186, 205
Valarian, Lady 95, 114
Valorum, Chancellor **39**, 115,
    169, 175
varactyl 28, 192
Veers, General **79**, 176
Ventress, Asajj 149
Veruna, King 174
Vos, Quinlan 7, 183

W

wampa 4, **193**
Warrick, Wicket W. **196**
Watto 44, 144, 147, 171,
    195
Wesell, Zam 62, **203**
Windu, Mace 60, 67, 103, **112**,
    178

X

Xizor 31
X-wing pilots **197**

Y

Yaddle 131, **198**
Yak Face see Saelt-Marae
Yarna **200**
Yoda 43, 70, 102, 109, 110,
    147, 183, 198, **201**
Yowza, Joh 202
Yoxgit **191**
Yuzzum **202**

Z

Zuckuss 5, **205**

ACKNOWLEDGMENTS

LONDON, NEW YORK, MELBOURNE,
MUNICH, AND DELHI

Editor Jo Casey
Designer Jon Hall
Additional Design Sandra Perry, Dan Bunyan,
Rhys Thomas, Toby Truphet, Lynne Moulding
Jacket Designer Owen Bennett
Managing Art Editor Ron Stobbart
Publishing Manager Catherine Saunders
Art Director Lisa Lanzarini
Publisher Simon Beecroft
Publishing Director Alex Allan
Production Editor Sean Daly
Production Controller Nick Seston

At Lucasfilm
Executive Editor J. W. Rinzler
Keeper of the Holocron Leland Chee
Image Archives Tina Mills, Stacey Leong,
Matthew Azeveda, Shahana Alam
Art Director Troy Alders
Director of Publishing Carol Roeder

First published in the United States in 2011
by DK Publishing
375 Hudson Street, New York, New York 10014

This paperback edition published in the USA in 2011

10 9 8 7 6 5 4 3 2 1
002–179615–June/11

Page design Copyright ©2011 Dorling Kindersley Limited.

Copyright ©2011 Lucasfilm Ltd. and. ™.
All rights reserved. Used under authorization.

Published in Great Britain by Dorling Kindersley Limited.

DK books are available at special discounts when purchased in bulk
for sales promotions, premiums, fund-raising, or educational use.
For details, contact: DK Publishing Special Markets,
375 Hudson Street, New York, New York 10014.
SpecialSales@dk.com

A catalog record for this book is available from the Library of Congress.

ISBN: 978-0-7566-8885-1

Color reproduction by MDP, UK
Printed and bound by Star Standard Industries Pte Ltd, Singapore

Dorling Kindersley would like to thank Clare McLean, Lindsay Kent for the Index,
and Emma Grange for editorial assistance.

Discover more at
www.dk.com